Prai

(almost)

"This treatise defines the faith and doubt dilemma experienced by every individual approaching their "defining moment". *"(almost)"* provides a subliminal camaraderie to those isolated in the paralysis of uncertainty."

-Quinn Stilletto
Artist and Educator

"(almost) is a triumph in creative writing, Egypt is a fearless writer that. If you are looking for a self-help book, you're in the wrong place. If you are looking for a unique insight on our faith and who we are as creative humans, you are in the right place!"

-Manuel Rodriguez
Vocalist and Poet

"(almost) is a phenomenal book that came into my life right when I needed it. Egypt is deep and insightful while still being down-to-earth and downright funny in her honesty. She forces you to look at your own life and rethink how you look at those (almost) moments."

-Valeska Parks
Author of *The Lost Apostle*
and *Children of Misfortune*

1

"*(almost)* is an engaging conversation with its readers. It is an honest look at what it means to embrace the feelings of expectation. Wondering what's waiting for us just around the corner when faith is all you have to go on. This book urges its readers to look at themselves through a sincere lens because that's the way God sees us. Egypt takes the reader on this reflective journey through anecdotal, and even funny, stories about her own life. Job well done!"

-**Biff Merritt**
Producer and Bassist

"Egypt has grown into a special young lady. To me, she's always been special. I am so proud be able to witness what she has morphed into from this tiny peanut (she weighed 5 lbs. at birth) into this wonderful 21-year-old. This book may take you from one end of the emotional spectrum to the other, but she has shown me that you will always come through the better for it. To me, she has never been "almost". She's always been there by my side. My baby."

-**Theresa Hill**
Grandma, Age 74

"It's ok!"

-**Noah P.**
Age Five

(almost)

EGYPT ALI

WITH A FOREWORD BY
BONE HAMPTON

Table of Contents

Chapter 6

Chapter 7

Chapter 8

Chapter 9

Chapter 10

Chapter 11

Chapter 12

Chapter 13

Chapter 14

Foreword

The phrase, "youth is wasted on the young" 100% DOES NOT apply here with Egypt. The manner in which Egypt uses her words and articulates exactly what she is trying to communicate is extraordinary. To say that this is an easy read would be misleading because as you will read you will never be unable to be inspired. You will automatically begin to process things in your life that you have just been ignited to rethink. The stories that she shares are both fun and thought-provoking. The way that she tells them is what makes you never want to put this book down. Bravo Egypt, for letting us into your world, while reminding us, that our worlds are not that much different.

- **Bone Hampton**
Award Winning Comedian

"Hallelujah nevertheless,
was a song that pain couldn't destroy"

    – *Joy Invincible*
Switchfoot

Together

We Will find

Home.

Almost

[awl-mohst, awl-mohst]

adverb

very nearly; all *but*

1.

This Is Not The Book
That You're Looking For

I'm not sure what kind of book has to begin with an apology, but this is one of them. I would like to apologize in advance for the simple fact that the book that you are holding will not contain the answers that you are looking for.

Not directly at least.

The most ironic part of that statement may very well be that I don't know who you are. I'm not sure what has led you to the point in your life where you have found yourself holding this particular piece of literature. I don't know that we've met, or what you're coming to these pages carrying. I also have no idea what it is that you think that you're looking for. Regardless, I do know this;

You will not find it here.

I believe that it is this search, the hopeful action of looking for answers, that continually drives humanity to a deeper level of thinking. It is the ever-present yearning for something more. It's the hope that answers lay somewhere just out of reach. The idea that if we simply keep reading, keep thinking, keep trying, that we will find whatever it is that we are looking for. There have been times where I have found myself searching for something. The problem was that for a while, I was not sure what that something was. Was I looking for the justification of my feelings, a sign that I was doing the right thing, or an interpretation of my thought process?

Whatever it was, I consistently found myself searching in all of the wrong places with all of the best intentions. I was staring at ceilings during concerts and hoping that the rafters could bring me the answers that my heart was searching song lyrics for. Looking for relationships that would fill a void that even I had yet to give a name to. Even then, nothing that I had found was exactly the answer that I was looking for.

All of the solutions that I ran into, and in some cases had accepted, only sort of solved the issue. They were close but not quite what I needed. This is a mistake that I think that we make all too often. In periods of emotional desperation, we place our hope and faith into something that *almost* fills us.

Almost

Almost is a hard word. In some cases, this one word brings up instances missed opportunity, near success, or half fulfilled dreams. It carries an indescribable weight in just those six letters. It is as though that one word is filled with the potential that clouds the eyes of hopeful wanderers but also holds just enough power to wipe that same wonder clean from their hearts. It is a concept that can be simultaneously be filled with longing, but also with satisfaction. It is representative of both the wait and the action. The struggle and the victory. It is also a term that demands with it some degree of honesty. So, let's start here:

I cannot pretend that I have all of the answers.

That in itself is a very strange thing to say in a book that I hope for people to read. I mean, isn't the whole point of reading a book to come away knowing more than you had before? Aren't these types of works supposed to be written and shared by people who know better than the average human? By some type of leader? The answer to that question may not be as satisfying as what you were hoping for. I am sorry that what you are looking for won't explicitly be contained in the following pages. I am not sorry that I could not be what was described in the sentences above.

Contrary to what my cat believes, I am not a leader. I'm actually not even remotely qualified to be writing this thing. I am a desperately broken being searching for meaning and answers just like you. In some ways, that can be disappointing. What then, is the point of reading the rest of this book? If I cannot provide answers to your questions, then why are we here? The point is that because I am just like you, we can work through this season together on an equal playing field. Through shared experiences, and personal revelations, I hope to be able to provide you with more questions that may guide you to what you're looking for.

Yes, I *want* you to have more questions.

This is also a strange idea in a genre of books that boasts about having all of the answers. However, this is the most important part. The promise of answers, especially in a topic as weighty as the concept of "almost", gives an illusion of knowledge and wisdom where none exists. It is a writer masquerading under the idea that they've found the path to enlightenment and resolution. I have only ever read one book that I am sure has those types of answers and

I'll give you one guess as to what that book is. The point is that I am entirely underqualified to provide answers with the amount of authority required to be taken as gospel. The crazy part is that even if I did, I would still be lying to you.

I just said that I did not want to pretend anymore. Can you make me that same promise as well? Can we promise each other that for the next hundredish pages that we can drop the mask for a minute? Call a pause to our charade and work to find our common ground?

I truly believe that the most dangerous thing that a human being can think that they are is alone.

The worst possible thing to think about yourself is that you are alone in your struggle, your journey, and your questions.

I promise you that you're not.

As the proud owner of a wandering heart myself, I can vouch for the fact that there is at least one-pint sized poet from Ohio that feels the same way as you do. The issue is that I can only speak from my experience and from the things that I know to be true. While I happen to think that this is pretty good footing, please do not confuse the anecdotes and stories that you are about to read as gospel.

It is my hope that together we can unpack this word and the season that it brings with it. By asking these questions and working to find their answers I hope to be able to help you find what you're looking for. It won't be easy, but you have already promised me your honesty and in return, I can give you my vulnerability. Those two things, when mixed with the right level of perseverance, create an atmosphere of healing. Only by coming into this conversation with an expectant spirit and a patient heart can we hope to make sense of where we are right now.

So, where are we exactly?

Chances are if you are reading this and have gotten this far, you like me, are in a season of almost. Almost is such a definite term for a finite amount of time. In so many cases we take its appearance in the sentence of our lives to mean a rejection from our calling. How much of your story starts or ends with the amount of times that you were almost able to go, be, or do something that just did not work out? How many times has this word opened scars of rejection, anger, doubt, and even fear in your heart? Nothing can be scarier or more uncertain than this season. It is the root of a lot of shady advice and bad ideas both in and outside of religious circles. It causes this almost toxic mentality of needing to give an appearance of confidence and superiority if only to hide how uncertain we really are underneath. That type of environment forces us to create a mask that is ultimately suffocating.

We won't be needing that here though.

Today is a chance to explore this grey area and give it some definition. An excuse to look at all of the doors of opportunity in front of us and to find some peace in the fact that some of them are still locked. To ask the questions that we've been praying for answers to and to be honest about how we feel. Most importantly, we can discover that it is ok to be here. That our stay in this season is not contingent on how good of a person we are, but that it is up to us to learn to grow in the wait.

Let's step into this grey area called the almost.

2.

Don't Listen To Me.

We Just Met.

I guess that this is the point where I should probably introduce myself. Hey, I'm Egypt. I'm a newly minted 21-year-old dreamer, who for some reason has been given the opportunity to tour the country as a cinematic spoken word artist. At its heart, spoken word is the art of performance poetry. It is the creation and the process of presenting a poem, story, or piece with a metered flow to listeners in both live and recorded settings. My particular form of performance also involves supplementary video and music components to aid in the storytelling. This means that I spend an awful lot of my time talking to myself. I like to say that my whole job is to make you feel something, even if that something is awkward. Some people enjoy telling me that I'm really good at that last part.

As a whole, my performance would not look too terribly out of place in a concert setting. This is a great thing as it is where I find myself most often. I have had the privilege of opening for some incredible artists and groups on events ranging in size from small youth groups to full-blown arena appearances. It has been insane to say the least.

The real mystery though is how exactly I ended up here. As a kid, I was, uh, difficult. Not in the context of behavior though. I learned pretty quickly that while the beginning of wisdom is the fear of God, the beginning of common sense is the fear of mom. No, the vein of difficulty that I found myself testing my mother with were my questions. Everything in my tiny elementary school life had to have a reason. Things like "yes mom, I understand I need to do chores, but why?", were common conversations. What did not help this was the fact that my mother was a lawyer. I not only learned persistence, but I also learned how to create factually founded arguments at a very young age. In short, I could argue with a stop sign and do so confidently.

My questions were my act of rebellion. I figured out that my words had the power to bring life to my family and then nag them back to death again in an instant. I thought of it as my very own superpower. My grandmother had another term for it though; the gift of gab.

This thought process followed me throughout my schooling and, I think, is what led me to my current line of work. All I wanted was to learn and then to use new information to challenge what I already knew. I treated my questions as my dissent, and in a way that made me a better writer.

Poetry in itself is an act of defiance.

It always has been. You can trace the use of the medium all the way back to the renaissance. It's easy to see that it has been used as a way to question the status quo. If a poet showed up to your event, and you didn't invite them, you knew you had trouble. I guess, in that way of thinking, I have carried on the tradition of poets before me. All of my pieces are questions as much as they are prayers. The content, generally speaking, always pushes the listener to question themselves as much as possible. This is also by design. I have never learned anything new without questioning old ideas, facts, or concepts. It is these moments of intellectual strain that often drove my classmates up the wall. Isn't it just easier to leave well enough alone? If it ain't broke don't fix it? Those are the sayings, right?

The issue is, I have just never heard of answers coming without questions being asked. There would be no such thing as a scientific breakthrough if an obstacle were not made known. There would be no reason for deeper conversations if challenges were never mentioned. There is no sense of personal freedom if the chains we are bound by are never questioned.

These truths are the reason that the idea of a season of "almost" is so difficult for me personally. For a kid whose entire existence seems to hinge on the question of "why?", being in a season of waiting is terrifying. It creates room for emotions like bitterness, anger, and doubt to come creeping into the crevasses that I had not yet filled with self- confidence and hope.

It becomes easy to move into what I call "emotional desperation" if spiritual confidence was never a skillset that we embraced in our everyday lives. Emotional desperation is the execution of decisions, choices, and actions driven by the need for a solution to an intangible challenge. It is the tendency to latch on to a problem without a solutions-based sense of thinking. It is exacerbated by pushing past all reasonable moments of peace in search of a resolution that brings an end to the problem. In many instances, cases of emotional desperation begin our seasons of almost.

Before we go any further, it is important to define what I mean by "the almost". Outside of being an incredible rock band, the almost is a season is kind of like the Twilight Zone. It is a place where any number of things are possible, but the environment itself is unnerving. It is this grey area between the state of preparation and the state of action. Here, your brain will tell you that everything that can go wrong will.

Acting in the type of faith that allows us to navigate seasons of emotional desperation and spiritual challenge is a skill. We can both agree that skills require practice to hone and perfect. The daunting part about practicing this particular skill sset is that the only environment where this skill grows is in times of distress and uncertainty. It is the same terrifying place that we found ourselves in when we asked "why?" to begin with. Once that question has been uttered, the location of the thinker becomes apparent. The season of almost is now front and center. While getting into a season of almost is easy, getting out of one can be complicated.

Sometimes the opportunities, events, and timing that mark the end of this season are beyond our control. It could be that job you've been waiting to hear back about, the finances you've been waiting for a breakthrough on or even that email that has kept you in suspense for months. Whatever the situation is, it's important to understand that a shift in mentality is needed in order to make sense of this season. We have to rid ourselves of our mindset that the term "almost" is synonymous with failure or the end of a dream.

Sometimes "almost" just means not yet, and we have to become ok with this. So often our frustration about our season of preparation blinds us to the idea that we are in fact preparing for something. We need to stop measuring our time of waiting against our worth as human beings. Our time of construction has no bearing on our quality as people. You are not defined by the time that you have been waiting. Your character can be measured however, by what you do during your time in your season of almost.

When I was younger, it was easier for me to get wrapped up in the ideas that were shown to me. I'm not sure where I picked up this thought process, but it was almost as if the world were telling me that my dreams were to be set in stone. That when presented with the season of almost, I was to buckle down and hold fast to what I wanted because only that will do. Moreover, that this seasonal stubbornness would be rewarded with all of the dreams that I had put my foot down for. This is not true either. Sometimes our seasons of almost are put into place to change our perspectives. It's there to do the same thing that I hope that my poetry does. I want to make people question things.

What if we are chasing dreams that would only destroy us in the long run? What if another avenue would be better suited to serve those around us? What if we are being prepared for the exact thing that we've been praying for, just not on the timeline that we set forward?

I cannot answer those things for you.

That's frustrating I know, but I really can't. I can tell you that from my anecdotal experience that I have been in a season of almost since birth. Or, at least that's what it feels like. As a child, my desires darted from wanting to be President to a strong passion for chemistry. However, I discovered that my gift of creating bonfires indoors was not normal or a celebrated one.

My dreams would then push me towards creative pursuits. Finally, in middle school I decided on a more nomadic life. I figured that if I could just become the guitarist for a band called Skillet then I could call it even. As you can see, Skillet has two phenomenal touring guitarists and neither of them are me. I'm not sure how well that one turned out, but a kid can dream, right?

I'm not sure whether or not my aspirations to be a touring musician will ever actually come to life. There have been so many "almosts" with that that it's painful. Regardless, I do know that I have been given the opportunity to be a touring poet. While it is a little different than shredding a guitar, it does give the opportunity to serve in a different way.

Serve

I've used that word twice in two pages, so I think the term also warrants a definition. What exactly does it mean when I say that I want to "serve" in what I do? As a Christian, I believe that there are gifts that are given to each of us from our Creator. What we do with those gifts though, is our choice. Using them to serve others in accordance to Ephesians 4:11-16, sounds like a good idea. Service in a role that could lead to the servant being in the public eye is a slippery concept. It was also something that I did not realize until recently.

I spent an unhealthy amount of time arguing with an audiobook in the fall of 2019. Mike Donehey's *Finding God's Life for My Will* to be more specific. Mr. Donehey is the singer for a band called Tenth Avenue North. One of my best friends just so happens to be one of their biggest fans. She talked me into reading his book on a flight home from Nashville. She went on about how funny it was and what a great read it would be. "You'll blow right through it," she said. "It's an easy read", she said.

I have never felt more lied to in my entire life.

Please don't misunderstand me, the book was great. I just did not sign up to be emotionally challenged by a guy I think I've only met twice. One of the first things that he tackles in his work is the idea of a servant leader. He argues that being a leader is simply not what we were called to do. That being a servant does not qualify us to lead people despite what we have been taught. I had never felt more attacked than in the minutes after reading that chapter. "What is he talking about?" I thought. "I have seen a whole bunch of servant leaders and all of them seem pretty cool!". Not only does Donehey go on to challenge the validity of the term "servant leader", but he also went on to proudly state that he doesn't want to be a leader anyway. To someone like myself who has always strived to hone my leadership qualities, this forced me to stop for a minute. Isn't becoming a good leader what we were all born to be? In that instant, he made me realize that I was wrong.

What I never took into consideration is that it is difficult to keep a servant's mindset while being pushed into a leadership position. While the two are not mutually exclusive, they do live in a paradoxical relationship with each other. A servant, by definition, is a person who is at the service of another. Their entire job is to create environments where those whom they serve can thrive. In terms of musicians and artists such as myself, our capacity to bring joy, reflection, music, and poetry to others would be considered an act of service. For me personally, I feel as though my artistry has been called to serve by bringing hope to those who need it.

What that does not qualify me to do is lead.

Now don't get me wrong. There are those who's act of service is their leadership, but not all leadership is an act of service. This is a mentality that can get people stuck in a season of almost. The idea that you can force a gift to be something that it's not, or to act on it in a way that was not intended, can cause quite a bit of strife between your spirit and your flesh. The important thing to know though is that this is a struggle that many find themselves facing. The outcome of that question though can only be debated and settled through personal prayer and petition. As much as I'd love to, I can't answer what your form of service is or what your gifts are.

I can only pose the same questions that I had to ask myself to you.

Often, I feel as though we look to people, events, and books like these for answers that they cannot possibly possess. We try and find answers about our own personal calling and purpose from people who did not give them to us in the first place. A season of "almost" can be triggered by these sorts of questions, and in this case, I think that's a good thing. Having the time to sort through all of these questions while in a season of preparation can be a blessing. It is like having the chance to map out a long road trip a week ahead of time. You would be able to double-check your route, find your desired sightseeing stops, and maybe even pick out the best bathroom break locations! If this type of outline wasn't prepared before you left on your adventure, then you would run the risk of haphazardly following your GPS along a route that you're unsure of. The amount of chaos and stress that would come from being unsure if you took the correct turn, and not being absolutely positive where the nearest bathroom stop is would be enough to ruin the entire trip. Instead, the preparation in the season of almost would allow for a much more comfortable journey.

That preparation is an intensely personal process. While it can be a great idea to ask others for guidance, it's important to know that only the Creator fully understands what the plan and purpose for your life is. He knows your entire being along with its questions and its quirks. He sees your darkest secrets and promises that His love is more than enough to cover it. Taking another human being's word for your purpose over that of the One who gave it to you is like taking candy from a stranger; Sure! It may sound like a good thing, but it's a terrible idea.

Do yourself a favor and don't listen to me.

Afterall! We've only just met.

3.

Uh,

Did You Forget Something?

When I was about six years old, I took my first trip to the local emergency room. I had been playing hide and seek with my sister. A chunk of wood peeled up from our hardwood floor and found its way through my sock.

It was not fun.

Given the fact that this piece of wood was pretty well embedded into my foot, and that I needed two of those to walk, I wasn't going anywhere without help. My mother had to carry me from our house, through the snow, and into the hospital waiting area. After waiting a while to be seen, a nurse emerged from the door and called my name. My mother, intent on making sure that everything was in order, got up and went to the door leaving me behind. I'm not sure exactly what I said to get her attention, but I'd imagine that it had to be something along the lines of "Hey! Are you forgetting something!?". She came right back to pick me up and take me to see the doctor. They were able to get the splinter out of my foot and I was able to skip PE for a few days. In all, I would call it an absolute win.

In hindsight, that moment in the waiting room revealed a lot more about my attitude towards the almost than I ever could have imagined. It is in moments of vulnerability and helplessness where we learn the most about ourselves. The immediate sense of panic at the thought of being forgotten when I needed help the most was paralyzing. It was worse than the pain that was happening in my body. It was a feeling that reached down into the very depths of a soul that I had not yet begun to explore. The only thing that I could do was to call out for help to the person who brought me there. Thankfully in that moment, the help was immediate. I could see where my mother went. I could also see her come back for me. In the season of almost, it's not that easy.

We can't always see the solution that's coming or know when the wait will be over. We can feel as though we have been left to sit and wait while longing to be made whole again. Praying that we can find freedom from our sickness, stresses, or other forms of challenges can feel like the ultimate season of almost. It is the space where our faith meets at the intersection of our expectations. At this crossroad, we stake all of our prayers and desires to all of our doubts and questions. Here we figure out which time can take first.

The waiting game here can be more agonizing than the end result. In this scenario, an immediate resolution at least brings some small sense of closure. Regardless of the outcome, the end to that period of waiting would be over, and with it the suffering that it produced. It would be easier to learn to live with those results if we had some inkling as to what those results would be. Sure, some of those answers would be difficult to hear and to cope with, but it would be an answer.

Sometimes, it is possible to confuse our desire for our time of waiting to end with our frustration in the process. In order to understand this concept, we would need to explore questions that may force discomfort on the unsuspecting reader. The reader who still has their guard up. The one who would rather have the mask that they've created will find what comes after this to be offensive. However, we have promised each other honesty, and I truly believe that reading this will be a process of healing for both of us. The simple answer as to why that waiting is difficult is one that would find itself scoffed at in most places of worship. In fact, I have seen people shunned for admitting less than this. The reason why the almost is so daunting is simple: It is not possible to have faith without exposure to doubt.

Sometimes our doubt is stronger.

One cannot exist without the other. Faith without doubt is just a fact with no opposition. The dilemma that doubt creates is the fact that it's sticky. Once it's got a foothold in one area of our lives, it spreads. It slowly envelopes everything that it touches until its bitterness and disdain mar even our new experiences. It forces us to look at our lives through a lens of jadedness. Take this as an example; How many times have you prayed for something, only to find that your requests went unanswered? How many times have you felt that you may have more of an emotional relationship with your ceiling than your Creator?

These questions make we as believers uncomfortable. It demands that we reevaluate our life choices and all of the decisions that have led us to this point of questioning. The time in the almost magnifies this feeling of longing. It aggravates our desire for answers and causes us to lay blame for the lack of explanation on the one who promised it to us. What if doubt was not just in the uncertainty of what we believe, but also our unwillingness to submit to a timeline other than our own?

I read a story on Facebook not too long ago that discussed in allegory the story of a man at an upscale restaurant. As the story tells it, this man was best friends with the chef. After the restaurant's opening day, the chef invited him to a special meal. This man had watched all of the great reviews from this restaurant. The fact that he had a personal invite from the chef himself was both humbling and exciting. The man dressed in his best suit and arrived on time for his reservation. The hostess seated him and promised that the chef was preparing a dinner especially for him with all of the trimmings. She served him water while he waited but warned him not to fill up on drinks as his food would be worth it.

As the man settled into his wait, he watched as others enjoyed their food. He saw how new diners were seated and placed their orders. As time passed, he grew agitated. He was hungry after all. He had also been invited. Why was it that the other patrons, some of whom had arrived after he had, were being served before him? He called a waitress over and told her about his invitation. He requested that she remind the chef that he was there. She assured him that the chef was aware that he was in house and was still working to prepare his meal. At this point, the man was starting to catch some strange looks from the other diners. Those who had already been served began wondering what the man was doing there at a table for so long. Some even began poking fun at him. The restaurant soon began to empty out and the man began to lose hope that he would ever get to eat.

At first, he was angry that he was being made to wait as long as he was. That anger turned to jealousy, and the jealousy melted into bitterness. Finally, he settled on the idea that he had simply been forgotten by the chef. He began questioning if he and the chef were really friends to begin with. He begins to question why the chef would stand him up the way that he had.

Just as he was beginning to gather his things and leave, the doors to the kitchen burst open. Out of them streamed four different servers carrying a plethora of food. Upon further inspection, this food was some of the man's favorites. The meal had undoubtedly been prepared just for him. The chef came out and sat with his friend explaining that he had been waiting for a special shipment of spices that he had ordered specifically for him. That he wanted only the freshest meats and vegetables. The chef finished his explanations by saying that had he rushed the meat, it would not have been as tender, or worse, undercooked. The man enjoyed his meal, thanked his chef friend, and went home.

There is a lot to unpack in this story aside from the obvious. None of that unpacking can be done without putting ourselves into the shoes of the chef's friend. I have been to restaurants with terrible service before and it's incredibly frustrating. It is so annoying to be so close to food, and yet so far away at the same time. To see what you came for being given to someone else and knowing that you still have to wait on your order? I cannot imagine how upset our fictional friend was here. At least on my restaurant misadventures, the wait staff have been strangers. It must have almost felt like a betrayal to have this same thing happen in the establishment of a friend. What I find interesting here though, is the idea that the man did not ask the waitress to remind the chef about his missing food order. He asked the waitress to remind the chef that he was still there.

Beyond the typical human desire to be fed, is the innate desire to be known. I said in the first chapter of this book that the most dangerous thing that a person could ever imagine that they were was alone. There is a reason for this that goes a bit deeper than an allegorical Facebook post. Being known simply allows us to have peace in the fact that we will not be forgotten. That someone somewhere sees us as individuals. That we are viewed as people with our own stories, hopes, dreams, desires, and fears. That to someone, we are not simply a face in a sea of expressions. That we matter on a level of understanding that allows us to be vulnerable.

The story never mentioned that the man gloated in the face of his fellow diners when his food finally did come. He was just happy that the chef remembered that he was in the building. That plea for recognition sounds an awful lot like my shout of desperation to my mother. The setting of a hospital waiting room sounds an awful lot like the setting of almost. We can only be made whole when we admit that we are broken. Often, we find that our most honest cries for help come when all other means of communication are exhausted. When we come to the end of our rope, we'll find that vulnerability does not require many words.

The second thing that caught my attention about this story was the idea that despite keeping the man waiting, the chef did not apologize. Instead, the man saw what the wait was for. Not only was his meal personalized, but it was also fresh. There was no out of the box solution for his problem. Every single one of his needs were addressed in the course that was brought to him.

The meat is what held my attention the most. I'm not sure how many cooks will end up reading this book but I for one come from a family with the gift of burning water. For us the idea of cooking anything is daunting. What I do know is that meat is known to be hard to cook well. There is no grey area with it. You either season it correctly or it tastes like cardboard. Grill it just right or it's on flambé. Most important of all, you can either cook it long enough for it to get done, or it can make you sick. Undercooked meat has led to the illnesses of hundreds of thousands, if not millions of people. It is a delicate art that I should never attempt. It is important to note that meat takes time to cook to completion. Rushing this process could have disastrous consequences. The explanation from the chef did not require an apology. The delay was due to him taking steps to ensure his friend's safety.

The same is true with our calling and purpose. It is so easy to get consumed by what we see others achieving or walking in. Sometimes we end up rushing our own calling. We would never want to eat undercooked meat, so why would we want a half-baked purpose for our lives? The season of almost may not be a place of preparation just for you. It could also be a place where you are so that your circumstances can be prepared for your arrival. You have not been forgotten in your almost.

Your plan just requires preparation for you to step into.

4.

I Lost A Fight With My Car

I try not to make a habit of fighting with inanimate objects. I really try to not make a habit of fighting inanimate objects that are both bigger and more solid than I am. If I had adhered to that rule though, we wouldn't have this story.

I bought my first car when I was 19 years old. It's a bright red, 2004, convertible. It's the type of car that my grandmother insists to this day that I have no business owning. She often jokes that nothing but trouble follows teenagers in convertibles. Now that I'm older I have to agree with her. While convertibles are great fun in the summer, driving one in the winter brings a new set of challenges. Given that I live in northern Ohio, this challenge lasts a good part of the year. It was a Saturday in March that would set the scene for my showdown with my vehicle. The day had already been a challenging one. That morning my grandmother had been admitted to the hospital for what was yet another health complication. My sister was away at school, my mother was at work, and I was left alone to deal with an empty apartment and a few needy cats.

I remember getting into the car that evening with what felt like the weight of the world on my shoulders. A huge snowstorm had just come through, blanketing my city in a near-perfect sheet of icy white flakes. To top this all off, my car's check engine light had come on for the 4th time this week and there was no heat. I had already taken it into the shop that day and was running low on funds to continue repairing it. However, desperate times call for desperate measures. That evening I could be found willing my little red convertible down slippery Ohio roads trying to get to the hospital.

I was trying to ignore the fact that this was the first snowy season that I had ever driven in. I made it to the hospital for a short visit and then began my slow journey back home. On the drive back, I started thinking. My winter tour was over, and while it was a good run, it was also a welcomed distraction from the number of health issues running rampant in my family. It allowed me a brief vacation from some other heart issues that I had been running from. Now that I was home though, there was no running from the uncertainty that awaited me.

I realized that nobody would be becoming by for a few days and that all of my friends were either on tour, halfway across the country, or busy. With grandma in the hospital and my mother working, I was hit with the sudden realization that once I got back to my apartment, I would be entirely alone. More than ever I just needed a hug.

You shouldn't drive while you're crying. Ohio winters complicate this further as tears turn to snow on contact with the air. In short, I needed to stop for a minute. I pulled over to collect myself under the guise of fixing up my road trip playlist. Tasha Cobbs had just released a new live version of a song entitled "This Is A Move". For some reason, I thought it would be great for my emotional state to listen to it for the first time right at that moment.

As this song kicked in, a friend of mine, who had landed himself on a much larger tour than I could ever hope to be on, called me. He was telling me excitedly of his adventures and about all of the new opportunities that he was being offered. He was enthusiastically talking about all of his newfound friendships. He ended the conversation rather hastily because he was about to get into a snowball fight with people that I only knew from YouTube interviews and greenroom door signs.

Don't get me wrong. I was happy for him. For me though, that only emphasized this moment of loneliness. That call brought attention to the fact that my car was filled with just me and every single one of my fears. It forced me to remember all of the things that I've ever wanted to be, and yet could never achieve. All of the rejection emails from every tour that I had put in auditions, resumes, and letters of interest for came back, and with it came the flood of questions that I had.

My awareness in my season of "almost" raced around my brain dragging with it that stickiness of doubt and anger. To make matters worse, Tasha was still singing in the background. The entire scene must have looked like something out of a bad soap opera.

"Mountain are still being moved" she sang.

Well, the mountains that I was looking at certainly felt more real than a vague struggle in a song. My mountains had names and they glared back down at my spirit in resolute stubbornness. Their titles were things like anger, defeat, and hurt. Those were very real adversaries whose conquerors did not yet have a title. I was at a loss with what to do with them, and they only seemed to be getting bigger as I came closer to having to deal with them.

"Strongholds are still being loosed", the song continued.

Have you ever gotten to the point where you are trying to hold back emotions that have been rearing their heads for a long time? I hated showing emotion.

As a kid, I would try and think about anything else to stop from showing anything other than stoic resolve. I'm not sure if I was afraid of being weak, or if I was trying to trick myself into being strong. Either way, it didn't work. That immaturity crept back up my throat as I thought to myself, "who even says the word 'stronghold' in a song anyway? Who does she think she is? Chris Tomlin?!". I had meant this as a joke, but it did nothing to stop the feelings that were about to manifest themselves in a pretty obvious way. I was an unwilling participant in an emotional event that was going to happen with or without my say so. "Whatever comes next," I thought to myself. "Whatever happens next is going to be all Tasha Cobbs' fault."

A few things happened simultaneously in this moment. The first was that my car's check engine light came back on. The ding that accompanies the light will forever be etched in my memories as one of the most stressful sounds I have ever heard. The second was that a picture of the above-mentioned friend came across my phone screen in a text message. In it, they stood smiling next to a venue that I've always wanted to play.

The caption read "wish you were here". The third is that Tasha Cobbs hit the pre-chorus of "This is a Move"

"God we believe, 'cuz yes we can see it,
That wonders are still what You do."

That was it. That line was all that it took. I wept in that moment in a way I'm not sure I ever had. Up until that point, my prayer life was oddly formal. I understood and respected the reverence and authority of my Creator. I was very careful of my words and in how I chose to speak with Him, but in that moment raw emotions controlled the unthawed part of my brain. There was no holding back. I looked up at the sky, punch my steering wheel, and yelled "God, can you see this?".

He must have because I was quickly introduced to His sense of humor.

My punch collided directly in the center of my steering wheel. As my fist connected with the rubber, my horn blared under the weight of my frustration.

That noise scared me so badly that I jumped straight out of my seat and hit the bottom of the steering wheel just as my seat belt yanked me back to earth. The top of my head collided with my door frame, and through the layers of snot and tears, I realized that I had just picked a fight with my car.

The pain in my head also told me that I had lost.

I collected what was left of my wounded pride and battered ego. I wiped the tears out of my eyes and quickly looked around to make sure that nobody had seen that. Then drove my flustered sense of self-confidence back home.

One of the most difficult aspects of "the almost" is the personal sense of loneliness that is experienced. We have talked about the innate human desire to be known by others, but sometimes being known by others does not help us when we do not know ourselves. Our frustrations in our seasons of preparation are usually inwardly focused. These emotions are intensely personal. In a spiritual sense, these same emotions may be viewed as dangerous. The challenge is that recognizing and dealing with our emotions in a healthy way is a part of the healing process.

Healing is also a step to getting out of the season of almost.

Our emotions become a problem when we lack the tools and understanding to work through them.

In order to sort out our emotions, we first have to figure out who or what they are directed at. Being flustered over a rejection email could carry with it a lot of targets. For example, you could be disappointed that an opportunity fell through while being angry at yourself, and jealous of the person who did end up with the job. All of that could be irritated by the doubt that has been cast on your self-confidence and the uncertainty in your future.

That is an awfully long list of powerful emotions to unpack. That conglomeration of things would leave anybody confused and agitated. Control over our situation comes with the ability to isolate emotions and work to find their solution in steps rather than all at the same time. This scenario, believe it or not, is a simple one. Things get far more complicated if the person that your emotions are attaching themselves to isn't a person at all. You could, for example, be frustrated with social constructs, systemic issues, or even yourself. While none of these things have a physical address, they are able to be given names and worked through safely. What I find challenges Christians, most often though, is when their anger, feelings of betrayal, and issues of trust are aimed at someone higher.

Did you know that it is possible to be angry with God?

I have no way of proving this, but I think that a lot of Christians are struggling with that. It is easy to compartmentalize negative feelings when those feelings are aimed at something that we have control over. With God though, we can't fight that. As Christians we are taught to have the utmost respect and reverence for our Creator. After all, we do owe Him our very existence, right? It has to be a sin to be angry with Him. Besides, I have heard of a guy who wrestled with God. He lost so badly that he not only broke his hip, he also needed a new name. Nope. I'm good!

One of the biggest reasons that a person can become stuck in a season of almost is their unwillingness to be honest about their feelings towards their Heavenly Father. Their prayer lives will touch everything other than the elephant in the room. Those underlying frustrations will taint the potential of the relationship. What God desires is a full relationship with His children. This does not mean that He is only looking for the parts of us that we have cleaned up and polished for His review. He is looking for our emotions. He would much rather you bring your anger and frustrations with Him forward in prayer than lose you to the bitterness of your heart.

Part of the art of vulnerability is allowing the One who should know you best, into your life at your worst. It should be comforting to know that He is already aware of what we are feeling. He did create our emotions after all. I'm sure that He is aware of all of their combinations and side effects. He wants us to understand that these things are a feature, not a bug. He is inviting you and your questions, all of your fears and your doubts, all of your anger and bitterness. He wants to have that conversation so that you can grow in Him.

Sometimes our seasons of almost are accented with the need to clear the air between ourselves and the One who led us there. I am thankful that I serve a God who would rather put me on the sidelines than lose me to the game. The first step to this process of reconciliation is honesty. If we're unwilling to admit our feelings in the privacy of prayer, how can we be honest about anything else?

This may take some time. Some of us may even need to seek the advice of a professional to work through our emotions towards both God and people. Some of us may just need to set time apart in our prayer lives to specifically seek that conversation out. No matter how it happens though, whether it be in the quiet, through some tears, or even a moment of anger, know that it is all a part of the process. Whatever it takes, set aside the time to pursue healing. Wounds tend to become infected if they are allowed to fester. Bitterness, anger, betrayal, and hurt are some of the easiest things to lose control of out of fear of confrontation. It is not worth your peace to hang on to a problem that is so easily dealt with.

Besides, I'm pretty sure you'd rather get it done in a way that doesn't involve you losing a fight to your car.

5.

This Is Not Where I'm
Supposed to Be

I was invited to my first real party when I was 19 years old. That may seem a bit late to a lot of you. Trust me, I felt the same way. In high school, my social life was almost nonexistent. While I am sure that there were some amazing parties, I was far too awkward to have been invited. I also had a habit of skipping school functions to go to concerts so that should tell you where my priorities were. When the opportunity to spread my non-existent social life's wings and fly came about, I was all for the idea. I found a nice dress, googled how to use various forms of makeup, and made my way to the hotel that this party was to be held at.

It was not long after my arrival when I realized just how far out of my league I was. I looked around and recognized faces that I had only seen in magazines and on television shows. As I tried to work my way into the door, I had to sort through members of the media who were waiting outside. They stood craning their necks to catch a glimpse of celebrities and recognizable faces. All of them hoping to get a last-minute interview. I was neither a celebrity nor remotely recognizable, but people on my left and right were being stopped and questioned. When I finally was able to get inside Nile Rodgers, like, the real Nile Rodgers, played on the stage to welcome the attendees. Anyone looking at me would have thought that my eyes had been replaced by dinner plates. I remember being frozen in awe at where I was standing.

This would probably be your reaction as well if the first party you had ever been to was a Grammy's afterparty.

That's right. I was a 19-year-old, wide-eyed, clueless poet, who had somehow managed to snag an invite to music's biggest night of the year *and* an afterparty. Trust me, I'm still asking myself how that happened. The entire thing felt like a dream from start to finish and I was determined to make the most of it.

Just the day before, I had arrived with my entourage in New York City. My motley crew consisted of my older cousin, my 73-year-old grandmother, and one incredibly excited poet. I had come back to the hotel room after the main awards show to freshen up for the party. After posing for pictures, my grandmother motioned for me to come closer. She gave me a hug and then held my face between her hands in a way that told me that she was about to impart some deep, existential advice.

"Be careful" she said sternly.
Then, almost as if it was an afterthought added, "and if you can't be careful, then be good."

Her words echoed through my mind as I stood on the first floor of the after-party. I was surrounded by hundreds of people. Some of them I knew, most of them I knew of, and then there were some that I did not recognize at all. In an attempt to pretend like I knew how to be social, I tried to strike up a conversation with people around me. The elementary schooler inside of me just wanted to learn and soak up as much as possible in those moments.

As I continued to converse with people, I noticed a trend. I chatted for about 15 minutes with an older gentleman about his cats. He mentioned that they occasionally make mixing music a challenge with their tendency to lay across his work desk. I, being a budding producer and sound nerd myself, asked him what type of music he created. He answered that he worked in the film industry as a composer. He went on to list a number of films I'm certain that you have either seen or heard about before finishing with "yea, I composed the music to those films".

Conversations like that went on for hours. It seemed like every time I turned around I was bumping into someone who could have held a master class in their field. Everyone had a business card, everyone owned a studio, everyone had a number one hit or multiple Grammy/ Emmy/ Tony wins. Everyone seemed to be a big deal. Everyone except for me.

I remember being hit with a wave of self-consciousness. I was suddenly aware of how different I was and just how underqualified I felt. Don't get me wrong, that night was one of the coolest experiences of my life. The entire lead up to the event and the awards themselves were an honor to be a part of. Every single person I met was incredibly kind and I made friends that evening who I still count among some of my favorite people.

The problem was that I was suddenly very aware of the fact that I didn't have all of their fancy equipment or accreditations. At that point, I had created all of my music in my bathroom. In talking to all of these people I was painfully aware of the fact that my biggest fan just might be my lizard. That moment was the first time that evening when I thought that maybe, just maybe, I don't belong here. Thinking of myself and my accomplishments in comparison to those I was standing with shot me right back to a season of almost.

That's right.

Comparison can begin seasons of almost.

Sometimes, the almost is a realm that we've pushed ourselves into. I have seen moments of action get sidelined when our feelings of inadequacy replace the faith that we have in our calling. Comparison has killed far more callings than failure ever has. It has the ability to point out all of our desires while tricking us into thinking that everything we do not have is the secret to what we want. Despite the fact that I earned an invitation to the biggest night in music, I was worried about all of the things that I did not know how to do. I had already lowered my self-worth farther than any one of these conversations actually would. The thought that I did not belong there not only detracted from the work that I had done to earn the invitation, it also diminished the word of a Creator who made the set of circumstances surrounding that trip happen.

While the words "This is not where I should be" can be an indicator of low self-esteem, it also can also be a sign of pride. The only way to determine this is by examining the posture of our hearts. This examination requires a degree of honesty that may take practice to gauge. As much as I'd like to tell you exactly where your heart is or the reason behind your season of almost, I can't. This is a question that can only be answered by you. It has to be looked at in all of the honesty that you can muster. Sometimes the truth is that our hearts are not in the place that we thought that we left them. Realizing this is ok, staying there is not.

Regardless of the space that your heart is inhabiting, this season of "almost" can feel pointless. In terms of belonging, it can feel as though we have either prepared enough for the action we are waiting for or like we are so woefully unprepared that no amount of time will make a difference. While this is a common feeling, know that this season always has a purpose. Whether that is to reset and realign your mission, to grow into, or even figure out your calling, know that this is just a season. No matter how you are feeling about this, I'm glad that you're here.

Let's grow together.

6.

Kitchen Fire(s)

Before I begin this story, I would like to make one thing explicitly clear. My family was born with many talents. My sister is an incredible basketball player, my mom's gift of gab is genetic, and my grandmother was a special needs educator for years. We do have quite the lineup of cool skills. The one thing that we were not blessed with was the gift of culinary excellence.

I learned at a very young age that our ability to burn water was something that was neither normal nor good. However, it was something that only my family seemed to be able to do. With that being said, you should know that my cooking abilities are a direct reflection of my heritage. You can blame genetics, you could blame my family tree, but whatever you do, you cannot blame this all on me.

In short, this story was not my fault

…

Ok, fine.

This story was not *entirely* my fault.

I set my kitchen on fire seven times in the space a single year. In my defense, not only does this seem to be a family curse, but I was also left at home on my own. My grandmother had left for a morning brunch with some friends and I was home from tour. I was also incredibly hungry. As a true American teenager, I decided that French fries were in my near future. As a broke American teenager, I also knew that I would have to cook these myself.

I chopped up my potatoes, poured some grease into a frying pan, and fired up the stovetop. In my hurry to eat, I spun the dial on the oven up as high as it could go and was greeted with an amazing discovery. I had no idea that our stove came with a built-in light show. Apparently, if you turn the heat up far enough, the stove coil turns bright orange!

Sounds amazing right?!

I must have slid the potatoes into the oil too quickly. The next thing I knew, my entire world was in slow motion. I was watching, with cinematic intensity, a wave of oil cascade out of the pan. The brown liquid curled at the top of its arch like waves on the ocean and crashed just the same. I soon realized the light show on my stove also included a pyrotechnics display. The grease collided with the coil. Flames burst to life on the burner and spread as the oil invaded the stovetop.

I'm pretty sure that this is the moment where the slow-motion cinematic effect wore off. My brain began to watch the story of my being as my life flashed before my eyes. The entire oven top was covered in fire. Never fear! My childhood had trained me for situations such as this. My mind raced to the one thing that I knew could combat fire. I knew exactly what I needed in order to stop this inferno; a cup of water.

Pause

My dear reader, I can hear you now. "Egypt, don't you know that you're not supposed to put water on a grease fire?" you ask. The answer to that question is very simple;

I do now.

It did not take very long for me to realize my mistake. In fact, the degree of my transgression was made almost immediately apparent. Where at first there were only flames on my stovetop, there was now fire *everywhere*. I grabbed the only thing that I thought could suffocate the flames; my sister's polyester blanket. I figured if something was going to burn, then it might as well be hers. I frantically started to beat the flames into submission when I noticed something rather alarming. I realized that polyester doesn't burn.

It melts.

Friend, let me give you a word of wisdom. There is only one thing worse than the feeling of molten polyester on your fingers. If you are already experiencing the above misfortune it means that this feeling may very well be in your near future. Yes, dear friend, the only thing worse than melting polyester on your fingers is the feeling of melting polyester on your tongue when you try to cool down your fingers. I let out one of those silent screams. I'm sure that I alerted most of the bats in the area that something was very wrong. You know this kind of scream. It's that silent inhale that comes when you split your toes on your bed frame, and then the emotional exhale that comes right after.

Yep.
Not fun at all.

I dropped the smoldering blanket on the floor and looked on in horror. The fire had spread to our new living room carpet. The same carpet that had just been laid down the week before. It was so new that just this morning I found myself rolling my foot across the floor. I knew that it may be the last time that it would come up not looking like an everything bagel. If I wasn't panicking before, I certainly was now. At some point, I did manage to put the fire out. Unfortunately, this was not until it had burned a hole into the carpet right outside of the kitchen. When I stared at this hole, my entire heart was filled with dread. The only thing that I could think of were all of the different ways that my grandmother could kill me when she got home.

Rather than laying down and accepting my fate, I decided that I had to at least try to clean this up. I scrubbed the walls and opened all of the windows. I threw away my burned potatoes along with the remnants of my sisters' blanket. I then washed the pan and waited. Soon, the only sign that anything had gone amiss were the holes in the carpet. Knowing that I couldn't hide that quickly, I stole the welcome mat from in front of our door and placed it over top of the carpet. After that, I did what any homeschooler would do when they don't want to be blamed for something. I went to my room and pretended to be asleep.

I do love my grandmother. She's an amazing human being, but she does have some qualities that make her rather, um, frightening. As I mentioned before, she was a special needs school teacher for decades. Teaching in Providence, Rhode Island during some of the most pivotal points in civil rights history made her a force to be reckoned with. She's 5 foot nothing and walked with a cane that doubled her wingspan. She's got a voice that can go from sickly sweet to murderous in moments. If that ever happened though, you knew you deserved it. She has the capacity the kindest human being that you would ever meet, but there is a reason that her kids and grandkids weren't known to cause trouble.

I heard her coming before I saw her. It was as though the "Imperial March" from Star Wars proceeded her entrance. Hearing the keys inside of the door lock was like hearing my doom approaching. She stepped inside and I heard her pause as though looking for something. Her footsteps faded and then stopped right where I knew the holes in the carpets were. Then they continued. I heard the sound of water running as though she had begun preparing dinner. At first, I thought that I might actually have gotten away with it. Then again, my thought process had proven to be rather faulty that day anyway. My relief was short-lived though. I heard grandma calling me from the living room.

Most people will understand this feeling. It is the sound that has plagued childhoods since the beginning of time. While I am sure that I have fallen victim to this moment, I know that I was not the first, and will not be the last. The moment that I am describing is that slow walk towards your parents after they have called you by your full name. Not just the first and last. I'm talking about that moment when your middle name is bellowed with the anger of a thousand suns and you know exactly what's coming.

I dragged myself out of my room and walked with my head hung low towards what I imagined to be my end. When I finally made it to the living room, grandma was seated on the couch next to the entrance to the kitchen. That same couch was also right next to the holes in the carpet that, oddly enough, were still covered with the welcome mat.

"Egypt, did something happen today?", she asked.

At this point, I was weighing my options. If I could get her to believe that nothing was wrong long enough for my sister to get home, I may really be home free. On the other hand, my grandmother has superpowers. She knows something is up and it's time to come clean. She sat and listened to my story of woe. As I spoke, I watched her eyebrow stretch higher and higher until I thought that it may disappear into her hairline. When I finished she stopped and took a breath.

"You're grounded" she stated plainly.
I opened my mouth to argue when she cut me off.

"You are not grounded because you set the kitchen on fire. This isn't the first time and it won't be the last. You are grounded because you tried to hide it from me. You can't hide the holes in the carpet from the person who owns the house". There wasn't much I could say after that. During my time in my room, I realized that my grandmother was right, but the lesson that she had taught me was much deeper than what she had intended. I stopped to think about the number of times that I had tried to hide other types of holes in my life. How many times have I tried to hide the holes in my heart from the God who created it?

It is incredibly easy to slip into the mindset that our mistakes need to be covered for. In a world where the highlights of our lives can be published for all to see, it is only natural to hide the rugged nature of our innate being from everyone, including ourselves. It is not possible to grow in an environment that is against the very nature of principled pruning. The intimacy of moral reconstruction is something that cannot be taught or practiced in situations where shame is more valued than healing. Our intrinsic inclination to be accepted will be in constant conflict with our need to grow in righteousness. To say that this is natural would be correct. To say that this was intended would not be true.

Shame is a powerful feeling. It's intrusive. It operates covertly in embarrassment and influences the agents of self-doubt. It invites criticism from others who are just as covered in this entity as the person that they gossip about. It, much like the essence of doubt, is sticky. Once it has a hold in a memory, it seeps into spaces that it did not originate until everything is coated in its presence. It is something that has been experienced by every single human being on the planet but is dealt with in wildly different fashions. The commonality of this occurrence is stunning, but I also believe that it is a poorly defined concept.

It would be foolish to think that all types of shame are the same. Some shame is rooted in situational embarrassment. I have spent many nights awake thinking about that one time I called my 3rd grade teacher mom or said "I love you too" to an unsuspecting pizza guy as I hung up the phone after placing my order. That type of shame, while difficult to work through, can be worked through in privet. I don't risk what little social status I have by admitting a mistake that may seem comical when explained to others. The type of shame that can be excused with laughter is one thing, but some forms of shame are different. Some shame can be toxic.

Certain veins of shame can find their origins in our desire to be seen as whole. We would like to be looked as though we are just as immaculate as the next guy in line. The problem is that our comparison is made against the precedent set by heavily edited Instagram photos and Facebook updates. We begin to portray our lives as though every attempt at emotional advancement is a confession of some deep-seated secret of inadequacy. Ironically, it is, but we as a collective culture view admitting our shortcomings as taboo. What is even more ironic than thinking that we must reach a level of synthetic perfection is the idea that anyone ever has.

When a season of almost is met with the distraction of shame, the two become potentially destructive. The developing sense of self-worth in an emotionally desperate individual may not be adequate in addressing the vulnerability that shame forces. It becomes a matter of time until the weight of ambiguity deforms the shape that a season of preparation is meant to take. It becomes far too easy to become complacent in a season of waiting if action means confronting visceral feelings of inadequacy. Societal pressures give way to emotional abnormalities if shame is allowed to dictate the appropriate level of vulnerability. It can be easy to feel as though the season of almost is eternal when the choice to be transparent is what separates us from our sense of manufactured holiness. The only way forward is to accept and trust a few key truths.

Firstly, we have to understand that everyone struggles. It's just a part of this journey. We are all a bit of a mess, and that fact alone is comforting. With that understanding, we can stop the charade of trying to look like we are whole to an audience of broken people. The holes in our hearts, like the holes in my grandmother's carpet, are repairable, but not through material means or methods. We cannot continue to patch God shaped holes with human sized alternatives.

The second thing that we have to grasp in this season is that we cannot heal from a wound that we refuse to acknowledge. By playing off our shortcomings, hurt, and questions we only allow the wound to fester. It becomes infected with shame, doubt, fear, and animosity in a season that is supposed to be preparing us for action. Infections in the spirit, like those in the body, have the ability to spread. Without acknowledging the problem, the toxicity of inaction will continue to wreak havoc in every other area of our being.

The almost is an environment whose very nature can exacerbate the effects of shame. Without a healthy mindset, it can easily drive us into the arms of comparison and back into this cycle of hole hiding that landed us in this chapter to begin with. The comforting part of this though is that our shame and shortcomings are no surprise to our Creator. He looks at our confessions and sees our hearts and promises that His love is still adequate. There are no surprises to the omniscient and that is much more satiating than anything that I ever could have cooked up myself.

I believe in a God who loves me despite the holes in my carpet.

7.

I Love Fishing But
I'm Terrified of Fish

The first time that I went fishing, I realized that I was really bad at it. Let's just say that the first trip ended with my hook stuck in someone else's nose and leave it at that. Despite the fact that I wasn't too great at it, I enjoyed the sport immensely. The great thing about touring is that I have the chance to try a ton of different fishing spots. Some of my favorite memories on the road have to deal with one of these adventures. I'm not the only one that suffers from terrible fishing skills though. Once a friend of mine took me with him and his family to go to a catfish farm. The idea was that because the fish were in an enclosed space, there would be plenty of bites. He was right, but while the rest of us caught pretty sizable catches, he only managed to bring in one half of a dead fish. We still aren't sure how that happened, but you bet your reel I remind him of that whenever I see him.

One particular fishing trip was more scarring than fun though. One year during summer tour, I found myself in upstate New York. The city that we were playing in was along a river that drained into a nearby lake. The locals bragged about all of the wide mouth bass that you could catch there. Seeing as we had some time between soundcheck and show doors, I grabbed my pole and travel sized tackle box and bolted for the pier. After setting up, I began frantically casting my line in an effort to coax some of the fabled fish of fantasy on to my hook. I must have been doing something right because within a few minutes I had my first bite. Instinct kicked in and I set the hook as I had been taught. Then I reeled in my prize. These fish were huge alright. That first bite easily topped my personal best wide mouth and now I wanted more. I continued to cast my line and consistently was getting bites on the hook. For a while, every time I threw the hook out, I'd reel in progressively bigger catches.

Eventually, the bites weren't as consistent. I started to get frustrated. I hadn't changed anything about what I was doing. The fish just weren't biting like that had been earlier. Finally, my phone's alarm went off and I realized that the show was getting ready to let audience members into the venue. I resolved to cast one more time just to see what I could do. I flung the hook as far out as I could and watched as my reel allowed more line to fly out of the spool. Once I saw that the hook had descended far enough into the water, I started to slowly pull the line back in. Not very long after that, I felt it.

A bite.

It felt different though, stronger. I started to get excited again. I imagined what could have been on the other end of my line. I feverishly cranked the handle on my pole to get my prize. The problem was that whatever I had caught was not cooperating. In fact, it continued to pull in the opposite direction. I tugged as hard as I could, but nothing I did made any difference.

I made a few mistakes in this moment.

The first was that I knew exactly what was coming, and I did nothing to stop it. I saw that the line on the pole was running low, and rather than cutting it, I dug my heels into the pier in an act of stubbornness. I'm not sure how stubborn it's possible to be in the face of something as definite as physics, but I was going to find out. The second thing that I did wrong was leaned forward to try and see what was happening. This comedy of errors meant that when the line finally did run out, there was very little stopping me from tumbling head over heels off of the pier and into the water.

Which is exactly what happened.

It felt like I was flying. There was this terrible moment where I could see both of my feet lift off of the ground and the pier behind me as I curled over in midair. I had enough time to pull a breath into my lungs and shut my eyes before the top of my head entered the water and I was surrounded by darkness.

I surfaced almost immediately to see the extent of my error. Luckily, I had left my phone and shoes on the hill in anticipation of what just happened. The only thing that got destroyed was my ego and my catch bucket which had been tipped over during my unplanned flight into the lake. My entire haul was escaping faster than the air out of my over-inflated sense of self. I was treading water as I looked for a good spot to get to dry ground when I felt it. Something incredibly wet, long, and slimy had just shimmed its way across my legs.

I have heard of people doing incredible things in moments of stress, but never did I think that I would experience it myself. After screaming loud enough to set off every sonar on every boat in the bay, I jumped so far up that my body was obeying the laws of LoonyToon physics. It felt like I shot straight out of the water and ran along its surface, screaming the entire time. In one motion I grabbed my shoes and phone then kept running. I didn't stop until I was back at the venue, soaking wet, and nearly in tears.

I must have looked ridiculous because before anyone on the crew asked what was wrong, they had to stop laughing. When I did finally calm down, I could only wheeze out vague details of a fish that had tried to eat me. The more that I recounted my story of terror, the more I realized that I was genuinely scared of the fish that just minutes earlier I was trying to catch.

I know that sounds absurd, but I really only like fish when I'm the one looking for them. In the same way, I only feel comfortable in circumstances that I can control, with variables that I am aware of. The almost challenges this frame of thinking. Comfort is usually the farthest word from our minds when we take to describing this season. In a lot of ways, life is like fishing. We work to prepare our life's tackle box with everything that we will need for opportunity. We practice casting our lines and when we are ready, we set off to the water and wait. From our fishing perch, we can see everything. We can watch where the signs of our goals are and see when we have a bite. We are in control when we reel our lines in and then celebrate our accomplishments as though we ordained the opportunity ourselves.

Until we get pulled in headfirst.

The moment that things stop being a part of the plan is when the season of almost begins. It is easy to operate in comfort because of the feeling of control and predictability. Complacency affords us the lie that the instability that we are chasing is sound. The second that our poles get ripped from our hands, and we tumble into the uncertainty is the minute that we begin to tread the waters of the wait. The idea that we cannot see what is around us or coming our way can be overwhelming. So overwhelming in fact, that the very thing we were chasing could cause us to run for the hills in retreat.

It is very possible to love fishing and be terrified of fish.

The chance at opportunity can be as scary as our season of almost. We have already talked about the stickiness of doubt and uncertainty. We have also talked about how the posture of our hearts affects the seasons that we find ourselves in. What we have not talked about is what happens when that season comes to an end. How do we know when we've walked out of our almost and into our destination?

As hard as this may be to believe, the line between preparation and action is not always as defined as you may think. It is possible to be so in love with the idea of whatever it is that you're searching for that you don't recognize it when it does appear. Some of us become so defined by our search that when the search is over, we become disconcerted by the lack of struggle. We can also become scared that we may not have been looking for the thing that we found.

There is something else about this story that I do still want to touch on. While my attempt at fishing was rather comical, it was a series of errors from start to finish. I was not really in any danger of falling into the water until I made my last mistake.

I refused to let go.

I looked into the unwavering power of Newton's second law of motion and told physics that I wouldn't obey. You can see just how well that one worked out. While the focus of fishing can be seen in the intensity of our cast, it is not the deciding factor in our catch. The decisive factor in our success is our ability to reel in the opportunity. The challenge is when we grip our insecurity in our calling so tightly that we choke out the timing that has been ordained for us. Not everything that comes past our hook is an opportunity that is right for our journey. Holding on to something that could overpower our foundation is just as dangerous as not having a foundation at all. Sometimes we hold tight on to hopes that we don't understand the consequences of. Occasionally we grasp onto things that could ultimately harm us because we are afraid of what letting go will feel like.

The fear of sliding back into the season of almost is also a natural one. While the time itself can feel like a defining moment, it is never promised that it will only happen once. That's a hard pill to swallow if you already feel lost in the season that you are in now. The comforting truth here is that growth will equip you for what you are about to walk into. I would much rather have the peace in knowing that I will have the resources that I need in the season that I am walking in. Without the blessing of an almost, I may run into position on a field I am unprepared for.

Yes, I did call the almost a *blessing*.

Though, I do have to admit that it took me a while to see it that way. I viewed the almost in the same way that I viewed my fishing process for a while. I thought that unless I was seeing results in my actions and dreams, I was wasting my time. That or that what I was chasing after must not have been in line with my calling. I viewed the word "almost" as a rejection of everything that I was working towards, despite what I knew my Father had led me to. It took a while to shift my mindset and view this time as the chance to prepare for what was to come, and to see that the almost can also be enjoyable.

Fishing, as it is on paper, should be an incredibly boring hobby. Actually, to some of you it still maybe. The idea that the entire point of the sport is to throw a hook as far as you can and hope that something bites sounds excruciatingly dull.

That's not all fishing is though.

Fishing is an experience. It is all of the preparation that preceded the first line casting. It is the time spent with friends. Even if you end up fishing badly by, for example, only catching half of a dead fish, you have a fun story to tell. It is coming to the water with the patient expectation of an opportunity, even if we have to wait for it. In the same way, the almost should be approached with the expectation of change on a spiritual level.

The moment that we begin to believe the lie that the place we are in is eternal is the point where we give up on our preparation. That is the moment that we settle into a life of complacency. We lose ourselves to the uncertainty of the waters that we find ourselves in and become scared when what we were fishing for swims right past us.

Do not fear the preparation or the length of time that it takes. It is different for everyone on every path.

There is no clearly defined way to get anywhere. No one lure entices every type of fish. Instead, take pride in the wait and learn to tread water in the meantime.

While it may mean that you aren't going anywhere in the moment, it also means that you aren't sinking.

8.

I'm Pretty Sure Getting Dropped on My Head
Gave Me More Common Sense

Let me set the scene. It is the summer of 2018 in Cleveland, Ohio. The sun is shining, there's a light breeze in the air, the birds are singing, and I was flying headfirst through the air in a parking lot. Just moments ago, I had been shoving my way through a crowd of rowdy concert-goers. I was dodging flying fists, and stray kicks from people much larger than I was. A giant circle had formed right in the middle of the crowd and in it were dozens of people pushing each other to the music. Crowd surfers leaped on top of the audience and were passed closer to the stage. Larger men and a few fearless women threw themselves against each other with frantic movements and curious smiles on their faces. The entire area of the audience was crawling with people, sweat, and optimistic aggression.

It looked like a blast.

I would say that I was thinking, but we both know that would be a lie. I had allowed my pride and heart to speak for my brain when I decided that I could take on one of the nastiest mosh pits I had ever seen. I squared up as the band playing hit a particularly nasty breakdown. The drums were heavy and rhythmic. The guitars screamed from their amplifiers. The lead singer shouted that he wanted to see that pit get rowdy. In response, the circle expanded, people on each side glaring at each other. I put my arms up and prepared to meet my maker with all of the excuses that I had as to why I thought that this was a good idea.

I'm getting ahead of myself.

Let's start over.

Have you ever heard of Van's Warped Tour?

Warped Tour was a traveling music festival that was in operation from the summer of 1995 to 2018. Usually consisting of mostly hard rock and metal lineups, the event was a hit for outcasts and shredheads alike. The festival hosted thousands of fans, served as career starters of dozens of mainstream rock bands, and was once played by Katy Perry. True story!

The events were usually held on festival grounds and parking lots. Several stages, a few dozen bands, and a whole lot of sweat in the middle of the summer. For any kid in the rock scene, attending Warped Tour was a rite of passage. It is the only place where I could have had lunch with a Satanist, an Atheist, and a Catholic all at the same time. Warped was the epitome of a musical melting pot filled with teenage angst and tradition. Playing any date on this tour was seen as a badge of honor to the rock music scene.

So, what on earth was I doing there?

Somehow, I had been selected to perform spoken word as a part of the line up on the day I went flying through the air. It is one of the most unexplainable parts of my musical career, but also one of my top 3 favorite performances. I grew up performing poetry on metal shows, so a lot of the lineup were groups that I knew of but never could dream of playing with. Some of them even became good friends. While I had attended Warped Tour before, I had never participated in Warp's most cherished tradition:

Crowd Surfing

Crowd surfing is the ultimate act of insanity. It is when an audience member jumps on top of the rest of the crowd and prays that they hold them there. The crowd then lofts the daredevil towards the stage and into the arms of some not so excited security guards. The view is amazing, and the feeling is unmatched. It's kind of like you're flying for the few moments that you're in the air. The trick is that once you're up there, you are at the mercy of the people underneath you. If they decide they no longer want to hold you, your flight turns into a skydiving lesson really quick. Make no mistake, they will drop you, but they will feel badly about it after.

On this particular day of Warped, I had just ended my performance on a side stage. I was over the moon about the opportunity and wanted to experience everything that the day could offer. I had just played one of the biggest shows of my life in my hometown and now I felt invincible. One of my favorite heavier groups had just started their set. As I heard their opening song a sudden thought struck me. After I packed my guitar up, I'd be done for the day. I had no further obligations and did not need to be anywhere else until the next morning. I had refrained from jumping into the crowds for fear of getting hurt, but this was going to be the last Warped Tour in Cleveland. I felt the sudden desire to live a little. Within minutes I had made my way to the stage that a group called Underoath was playing. I became a whirling dervish of emotions and limbs as I crashed into anyone who didn't move fast enough. At first, I couldn't understand why people did this, but once I started it was kind of fun!

Well, it was fun until I got punched in the face.

I'm sure it was an accident. I am pretty short, so my nose is at about fist height to most people. The problem is that that hit sent me reeling. I crashed backward and in trying to correct my fall, ran headlong into a rather, uh, large gentleman.

I hit him so hard I bounced off.

In the absolute chaos of the moment, I ran towards the edge of the pit. A couple of guys on the edge of the fray moved to meet me. I couldn't hear a word that they were saying over the music. The pit behind me was just getting more frantic. One of the men motioned towards the front of the stage. I could have sworn that he had mouthed the words "Do you want out?" to me. I quickly nodded as I felt more people pushing around behind me. I stepped towards the pair thinking that they were going to let me through. They turned their bodies in what looked like an effort to let me escape. It turns out the word "out" can easily be mistaken for the word "up" when you can't hear a thing. Instead of letting me through, the two grabbed both of my arms and legs and heaved me skyward in one smooth motion. I was suddenly flat on my back staring at the clouds, supported by the crowd below.

I twisted over to look at the stage. Spencer Chamberlain, the band's lead singer, was having a blast. I kept getting closer and closer to him, and for a moment I imagined the magical moment when our hands would meet in the ultimate high five. It was as though he read my mind because all of the sudden, he started towards me, and our eyes locked. I started to reach for his hand as he came over the barricade.

"Holy cow," I thought.
"He's actually coming over here!"

Unfortunately for me, I was correct.

I will never know what he was trying to do. He jumped off of the stage and was standing on the barricade in the spot I was headed to. Looking dead at me, he stepped on top of the rail and reached. All I know is that as I reached my hand towards his, Spencer crashed on to the front row in his own attempt at crowd surfing. Let me tell you something;

If a crowd has the choice between holding you and catching Spencer from Underoath, they will always choose Spencer.

It's nothing personal. It's just the truth. I came to this conclusion as the crowd underneath me reached towards him. My head dipped before my body did. To their unending credit, a member of the audience did catch my legs, effectively tombstone pile-driving me into the pavement. Not to be deterred, the audience picked up the parts of me that had pancaked into the ground and continued to pass me forward if only out of obligation.

The security guard who caught me immediately asked if I was ok. I'm not sure if it was the concussion or the heat talking but all I could do was laugh and nod. He set me down and I continued with my day, albeit a little slower.

The thing that the almost is very good at is making what we see look like what we want. There was not one shred of a good idea in my joining a mosh pit. The very concept of a mosh pit is a bad idea. While unloading aimless aggression is healthy, doing so by punching somebody else is not. This is exactly what we do in moments of emotional desperation and spiritual immaturity. How many times have you caught yourself doing something self-destructive in the hope of relief? How many band-aid solutions have you repeated without solving the actual issue?

Your band-aid solutions may have different names. Some of them may be an addiction, self-harm, or substance abuse. The things that we do to mask the core issue are not a sustainable method of coping. All that it really hides is what has driven us into the mosh pits of our lives to begin with;

Chaos

For some of us, chaos is a constant feeling in our lives. It is the ever-restless need to move when stillness is the only thing that will bring us answers. It churns powered by our anguish and angst. It will masquerade as normality while simultaneously telling us that we are the only ones in a season of struggle. It can lead us to a place of loneliness in rooms full of people. It is a mosh pit of thoughts, ideas, and negative feelings that can be overwhelming if not handled correctly.

Chaos also has a way of magnifying the manufactured peace of others in our minds. In our seasons of conflict, it is easy to look at those things floating above us and point to them as the embodiment of what we think that we need. It is easy to look at the crowd surfers and see stability when we can't see what's holding them. While they may seem weightless, the truth of the matter is that they are just as likely to hit rock bottom as we are in that moment.

This knowledge is only discovered when we chase the things that we see above us. We run into the fray and willingly or unwittingly end up getting tossed into more turmoil. The worst part about chaos though is that we don't know that we are headed towards it until we get dropped. By then it's too late. We hope to have moments like the crowd surfers at Warped Tour. We don't realize that if our hearts become distracted by another burden, we can easily get dropped headfirst into the fray that we just tried to escape.

Not only do we suffer the unsettling environment of the season chaos we got plopped in, but we also are hurt from our fall. It will be easy, in the event that these things do come to pass, to forget that there is more to our struggle than the pain that we experience. Struggle builds endurance, and while it is not fun in the slightest, it also builds and cultivates the resources we need to cope. Holding onto the idea that there is an end to this fight can be difficult to remember, but here is a promise;

Pain may be what led you here, but love will be what leads you home.

I cannot tell you what the reason for your season of almost is. I also can't tell you why so much of it feels chaotic. What I do know is that there is one constant in the storm that you are facing. That is the fact that true love is unconditional. I'm not talking about the Disney princess type of love. There are no fairy godmothers and no enchanted clocks that I am aware of. Last I checked, there were no singing animals on this side of eternity either. If there were, I'd think that we would have some bigger concerns than just the chaos in our lives.

This type of love is persistent. It pursues us in our mess and finds our potential in our chaos. It looks at our struggle and decides that it wants to fight with us too. It stares at our mistakes and comes to meet us anyway. It is constantly calling us to live in a type of peace that we cannot know without an understanding of its grace.

It is hard to understand peace if you have never truly experienced it. Overall, I think that is exactly what the almost is; a lack of peace. That can be peace in our calling, peace in our waiting, or peace in our own skin. Either way, we can be robbed of peace in our struggle. The fight between our flesh and our spirit is to take exactly that. It wants to rob us of our composure

To combat this, it is important to find tranquility on a solid foundation of love and understanding. It is the act of giving ourselves the space to accept our feelings and work to change them. To stare at the chaos in our lives and proclaim that it will not own us. It is the choice to believe in something more than synthetic serenity.

The almost has the capacity to be filled with an uncanny amount of chaos and comparison. It forces us into seasons of waiting that are only ended when we fight our urge to fight in the first place. It is setting our weapons down, bringing our insecurities to the altar, and allowing it to alter our mindset of longing.

It is easy to stay in an emotional state of anger. Not only is it natural, in some cases it is expected. Our circumstances and the grey area in our lives sometimes come at the cost of our patience. The struggle is natural, but understand that peace is a choice. It is intentionally seeking out time to collect our thoughts and rally for another day. To concentrate on a way out of our fray rather than why we are there to begin with.

It is the opportunity to accept a love that has pursued us from our birth through our mosh pits.

9.

This Is Why
We Don't Listen to Jason

....

Jason is an incredibly talented kid from the southwest of the United States. He's a member of one of my favorite sibling groups and in a really cool band. Jason is also a very, uh, special boy. Don't get me wrong, I love the kid to pieces. I just won't ever listen to him again.

Jason's band was opening for me on one of my headlining runs. His group consisted of a bunch of high schoolers, one of whom being his younger brother Dylan. On a day off, we stopped at a mountain somewhere in Arizona. Being the adventurous crew that we were, we set our sights on climbing to the top of the iconic Bell Rock. With a summit elevation of 4,919 feet and an asthmatic me trying to climb it, the day was full of adventure.

Dylan and another boy in the group took off as quickly as they could at the base of the mountain. The pair of boys darted in and out of view, around cactuses, and up the side of the terrain. Not to be outdone, Jason turns to me promising to know a quicker way up the mountain.

We need to pause here.

You should know that as a proud city kid, this entire experience was already incredibly far out of my comfort zone. I love the great outdoors! I just think that it pales in comparison to the even greater indoors. When I was told that the day would consist of hiking, climbing, and in my case stumbling around a mountain in the Arizona heat, I was excited! Until I was actually doing it. I do have an excellent sense of adventure. I would just much rather the great outdoors be left to National Geographic.

With this hesitation in mind, I skeptically followed Jason around the side of the cliff face. He was talking excitedly about how we were going to beat the boys to the summit. He was so confident in fact that I never noticed that we weren't actually getting any higher.

We got about 45 minutes into our wandering when I began to question our tour guide's qualifications. I asked him where we were going, and he continued to point upwards. He reached an opening in the path that I could have sworn that he was creating as we went. He encouraged me to climb. I tried first, and it did not go well. This side of the mountain was not made for climbing. My fingers slipped and I fell backward. Jason tried next and had similar results.

"Jason... Do you have any idea where we're going?" I asked, already knowing the truth.

The answer was evident by the look on his face. We turned back around and picked our way back to the foot of the mountain. The time that we had to climb was running out, and our little deviation from the path had eaten up our opportunity to reach the summit.

I teased him the entire way back.

I make it a point to remind him of this incident almost every time that I talk to him. I now refuse to take any directions from him. I wouldn't trust his advice about which shelf the milk is on in the refrigerator anymore than I would trust him to lead me up a mountain. It's not that he got us lost. I can forgive faulty directions. It how confident he was while he was getting us lost that astounds me. I'm sure that he started with the best of intentions. His mind's eye saw adventure and his ego heard his brother bragging about how was going to beat him to the top of the rock. I am guessing that the combination of his bravado and his adolescence is what led us here.

It's funny how that works isn't it?

It's almost amusing that our pride has the ability to lead us to places that we cannot find our way out of. It not only has the propensity to keep us there, but it also fuels our unending drive to reach a dead end as quickly as possible. We push towards the target that we have put our sights on, regardless of if we know how to get there.

What is pushing that drive though, is different for everyone. Are we pushing through our season of struggle in order to keep up appearances to our friends? What if we only want to look as though our season opportunity is unending because a season of almost is not as appetizing to our social media feeds? After all, I am not sure that I've ever seen struggle be glorified in the arena of likes and comments, where our numbers dictate our relevance. Even artists and bands are even encouraged to continue the appearance of activity in order to seem never to have downtime. This attitude is neither healthy nor helpful.

In fact, it's toxic.

Not all parts of the almost are tangible. Not everything about this season is a visible struggle or opportunity. Some of it is an emotional setback. While periods of waiting can be triggered by both of these things, sometimes the almost is triggered by our need to continue "doing". It is as though we are only worth as much as we can do. Meaning, if for some reason we ended up doing nothing for a time we feel like our worth the humanity is the same.

It is possible to replace our true identities with the ones made for us. Rather than valuing our worth in the light of our creation, we view it in comparison to what others may think of us. By giving into this notion, we allow our hearts to lead us into the wilderness of unfettered fears and pride. We consider it to be a matter of moral incompetency to fail without considering what failure actually is.

Failure is an opportunity to learn.

It is the chance to correct past mistakes in order to create a better tomorrow. It's a chance to allow ourselves the chance to grow, without the shame of onlookers to hinder the process. The almost is our opportunity to iron out our character, morals, and conduct before we are placed into our season of action. Do not despise a deficiency in your knowledge base when the season of almost is giving you the opportunity to learn.

I may not listen to Jason anymore, but that kid has grown more than I could ever describe by understanding what the season of almost gives in terms of opportunity.

He's going places. Maybe not to the top of Bell Rock, but places!

10.

No Mom,

There's Not a Dying Moose In My Room

I'm Making Music

I began producing my own music around the time that I started to release poetry records. I didn't know what I was doing when I started. Quite frankly I still don't. All I know is that my skills are heads and shoulders over what they were.

The first few months were ugly.

I did not have help when I first started. I don't say this to astound you with my progress though. I say this so that if by some chance you come across some of my earlier recorded poetry, you don't judge me by it. I did my absolute best to scrub the records from before 2015 out of existence. Every once in a while, one finds its way through a meet and greet line or onto Instagram and I cringe. I legitimately wonder how I was able to make it to where I am now seeing as people actually heard these projects. I promise you, if you had heard the first few works of mine, you would be wondering the exact same thing.

It took several years, a good amount of practice, and the patience of several real producers to make me sound almost competent. I spent hours on YouTube and shadowing others to make up for my lack of experience. I will always be grateful for the fact that they somehow saw hope for my future as a producer regardless of my total lack of skill. Despite my early ineptitude in the art form, I did grow to thoroughly enjoy the process.

The art of creating a melody from nothing is an interesting one. There is no one way to approach it, and no right way to go about it. No matter how it ends though, it will always begin with an idea. That idea could be a feeling or a beat, but it's what happens when you build on it that is magical. You could give one hundred different producers the same chord progression and you would end up with one hundred different finished products. Each work is built from the ground up and contains the identity of their creators.

They don't always sound beautiful though. Sometimes the beginning of musical genius sounds like the ramblings of a mad man. Once, I was working to create a melody line for a song idea that I had. I hammered out different ideas through a variety of sounds that were stored on my computer. I thought that it was going pretty well until my mother asked me why I was watching Animal Planet at such a loud volume. I paused what I was doing and poked my head out of my door to ask what on earth she meant. "It sounds like there a moose dying up there or something!" she called.

Well, that was humbling.

While I was just a little offended, I had to respect the part of the process that I was at in my production. Yes, parts of my home-brewed creations did have the tendency to sound like absolute death to begin with. There were times where I am positive that Bob Ross himself couldn't have found something redeemable in my mixes. The thing is if given time there is something beautiful that can be mined from the ashes of my attempts. With enough coaching, pointers, guidance, patience, and work, it was possible to create something beautiful. To allow the mistakes in the melody to meet in one harmonious accord to create a song. This anthem of brokenness would then hold the potential to change hearts, speak life into its listeners, or annoy the living daylights out of my mother. If it's a song that I created, then I'd hope that it is a balanced mix of all three. The point here is that production is a process. The act of creating, shaping, or improving anything meant to have a purpose is a long one.

In the same way, the almost is also a process.

Our lives are melodic in nature and dynamic in season. Our stories sing songs of triumph and struggle while pushing forward in their movements. Each act progressing farther than the last. Each passing event in our lives leaving a note to be replayed by those that come after us. It is possible to weave ourselves around creation, creating songs that may not be the most pleasing to the ear. We all make mistakes and struggle, but that doesn't mean that the minor fall in our progression is to be the end of our musical work.

At the end of the production process, producers typically take their musical tracks and songs to a place where they can test their work. If all of their songs are only ever played through studio monitors and speakers, then they'll never understand what everyday listeners are going to hear in their headphones. For some, this place can be their personal computer speakers. Some people share the mixes with friends. I usually find myself in my car. Car speakers have the tendency to be rather unforgiving. If there is something wrong with your song, rest assured your car radio will let you know about it in short order. It amplifies the inadequacies in the project and sends you back to the studio with a page full of notes that you can improve on.

If you think about it, the almost is the ultimate car radio test. It is a space where if only for a moment we are kept in waiting, surrounded by the noise that we make. Sometimes what is echoed back at us could use a little work. The rough draft of our existence gives us notes as to what we could continue to learn and areas that we can improve on.

At this point, we have a choice about how we can proceed. We could continue in our season of almost without working to improve ourselves, our skills, and our outlook. This may not be the best idea, but it is the easiest. The other option is rising to the challenge of change. To listen to the mix of our lives and decide that working on our process is worth the harmony that we have the potential to reach. It may not be pleasant, but revisions guide us closer to everything that we have the capacity to be.

We all have the chance to live our lives like a song,

11.

The Cat Called Fish

I got a new cat recently. Well, she's new to me anyway. She's actually adorable. A multi-colored calico who loves snuggling more than life itself. She was a cat that my mother took care of before she moved from away from my childhood home. When it seemed like she may not have a place to go, I moved things around so that I could take her in myself. When I got her home, it was time to pick a name. I watched the way that she acted around her water dish, drinking as much as she could whenever she could. I settled for calling her Fish, as in catfish, and called that a day.

She was perfect for me. Her incessant need to cuddle only made her more endearing. Her complexion makes her incredibly photogenic. She's even got an Instagram account. She enjoys sitting anywhere that I am, including across my desk while I mix music. It never mattered the volume. She could always be counted on to be there. I'm not sure why I did not find that fact odd. Usually, cats are very skittish. Fish never did startle easily.

Actually, Fish never startled at all.

I can carry her around like a football. She doesn't seem to mind. It's as though she just wanted to be near me. At night, she would walk along the side of my bed and crawl up to the entrance of the blankets to sleep on my pillow. She is the most canine-like feline I have ever met. Sure, she's a doofus. She has a thing for running into walls and refuses to move if I came up behind her. I just chalked this up to stubbornness. In all she was and continues to be one of the most amazing animals ever. It wasn't until 3 months after initially getting her that I noticed something was wrong. I'm really not sure how I missed it, but once it was confirmed it was obvious.

Fish is deaf.

I have no idea how I hadn't seen this before, but it was true. I cradled her in my arms for hours after this shocking discovery was made. I snapped in both of her ears in disbelief and watched as she did not react. I tried sneaking up behind her and startling her, trying to force her to hear me. Nothing worked. She really was deaf, and I had missed that for months.

As it turns out, all of her little quirks were caused by her struggle. She enjoyed sitting on my desk while I worked because she could feel the vibrations of the music. Her refusal to move as I walked behind her was not out of stubbornness. She just didn't know that I was there. She enjoyed snuggling not because she wanted to be in the way. She wanted to feel safe and loved.

You should know that you have friends like that.

Most of this book up to this point has been introspective. We have laid down the precedent that the almost is an intensely personal place. It's this grey area between our preparation and action, full of chaos and struggle until peace becomes our target. What we have not yet talked about is what this struggle looks like in others. Sure, they may not literally be deaf, but I promise you that some of your friends might be fighting some of the same uncertainty that we have discussed here.

One of the most amazing things about people in general is the fact that each and every single one of them are their own story. A completely unique snapshot into a complicated history of circumstance. They are the product of an ongoing process, still processing their emotions in real-time. Every single person you meet is in the middle of their own story. Purely by coming into contact with them, you have the chance to play a part in their process. Will you be the hero or villain, an NPC or a side quest? Will you be the shining hope of a better tomorrow or a reason for a season of almost today?

That's all entirely your choice.

Please do not misunderstand me. It is not your job to fix anybody. That is an impossible task that is only destined to drag you to a place darker than the failure that awaits your attempt. I am just saying that it is important to remember that the almost is challenging. It affects every inch of a person's existence. They, like my cat, may just need a little extra love. A genuine compliment, an honest smile. The feeling of acceptance in this process can go a long when you think that you're alone.

Make sure to check on your strong friends. Remember, some masks are harder to identify than others. The almost comes in many shapes, sizes, forms, and timelines. Love and grace are the only forces powerful enough the break that cycle of thoughts that remind others of their seasons of struggle. You have the chance to ease this.

Be the person that you needed in your season of almost.

12.

DUHN duhn

DUHHHNNNNNNN

If you didn't read that chapter title in a way that sounded like the intro to a dramatic horror movie, then you're doing this wrong.

One a brisk October day, a few friends and I pulled up to a field in the middle of nowhere Ohio. We heaved ourselves out of the car and stood, looking at the entrance to the scariest haunted house in the state.

That's what the advertisement called it anyway.

At this point, it just looked kind of comical. It was a series of seven different houses. Each was supposedly more terrifying than the last. After purchasing your ticket, you were supposed to join the line of haunt goers and wait to get into the first house. The last room of that house would then lead to the line of the next. The idea was that there would be no break in the houses. Just finishing one did not grant you a reprieve from the terror that you paid for.

I was not convinced.

My motley crew joined the line to buy our tickets. As we waited, teenagers with theatrically gruesome chainsaws snuck up on unsuspecting patrons. My head was on a swivel, constantly scanning the area for ghoulish pranksters. I refused to be the member of our group that got pounced on by a vampire. My pride just would not stand for it. I could not let that happen.

After we bought our tickets, we were told that we would earn a special hole punch in our ticket for every house we completed. If we could make it through all 7, then we earned a coupon for a slice of pizza at a local shop. We joined the line for the first house. Every once in awhile, I could see people running back down the side of the lines. This was odd. The idea of this particular haunt is that each house would come in quick succession from the last. You weren't supposed to see those who went in before you, as they should be continuing in the gamut of houses. Despite this fact, people continued to come past us, back towards the attraction's entrance. As I passed a staff member, I asked where those people were coming from.

"They chickened out," he said.

"The only way out of these houses is to push through to the end, or to come back the way you came in."

This wasn't reassuring. A few people came running out of the side door at a full sprint. They didn't stop until the made it about mid-way through the queue. Here they collapsed into either laughter or tears. I looked at my friends, and then forward at the waning amount of people that separated me, from whatever they were running away from.

If you've ever been in a haunted house, then you'll know that you do not ever want to enter a room first. For that reason, I shoved the only other girl in my group ahead of me. If anyone was going to get scared, it was going to be her.

The first house was entirely empty and pitch black. We were given a small flashlight that didn't quite work and instructions to keep moving forward. There weren't any scares in this house, but there didn't have to be. The isolation of the inky blackness and my imagination were quite enough, thank you very much. The second had a zombie theme. I found out that the zombies couldn't run very quickly. Maybe it was the fact that I ran, screaming murder, and slamming every door that I passed. Either way, they didn't seem very interested in following.

The third, fourth, and fifth house passed without incident. The sixth house however, scared me to pieces. At one point an evil nurse appeared from around a corner that I was not careful enough to check. I saw her and shrieked loud enough to eclipse the music playing in the attraction. In the same moment, I leaped into the air, and in my terror forgot how to use my legs. I fell backward and crashed to the floor in a wailing mess of my own making.

It took several moments, and the nurse leaving before I could collect myself and the shreds of dignity that I had left. We made it out of the house as the others laughed at my expense, though they were also clearly shaken. When we turned towards the final house, we knew that it would be different. The last house was supposed to be the scariest. I could not imagine how badly this was about to be for me.

The last house was set to the theme of a butcher's shop. There weren't many videos of it on the internet, but I did know that this house has the highest rate of dropouts despite it being at the end of the haunt. I could hear heavy metal music blaring on speakers inside of the house. I could see people streaming out of the "chicken" exit. Some of them were shouting swear words that I'm sure Tim Hawkins wouldn't approve of. Others just sat down once they hit the night air. Regardless of the reaction, I knew that whatever was in here was not going to be good.

We had already come so far. I promised myself that I would not use that chicken exit. I was going to make it through. I joked that maybe the guy in the group should go first. He volunteered, though he will claim that he was coerced.

I'm not saying that he wasn't. I'm just saying that he didn't put up a fight about it at the time.

I brought up the rear of our crew. I was thinking that if anything did jump out, I would only have to outrun one of them. If I was the least surprised by whatever caused the people in front of me to panic, then I stood a fighting chance at not ruining my perfectly good pair of pants. This worked for the most part. The last house was longer. Different performers leaped out at us from all sides. Every room that we opened held new horrors, but I was always alerted by the people ahead of me.

Everything was going well until I heard the chainsaw.

I think I may have marked my territory a little bit in that moment. The sound was coming from directly above my left ear. Whoever was there had snuck up behind my group and was now chasing us through the house.

I lost my *entire* mind.

The guys in front of me had already made it out of the next door, but in my haste, I tripped and skidded across the floor. I sat there in terror. I was too scared to scream and too stupid to move. I'm not entirely sure how long I sat there, but it was long enough to come to peace with the fact that this was going to be how I died. At some point, a hand gripped my arm and pulled. I resisted at first. There was no way I was going to go through any more rooms. My eyes darted around for the chicken door. Before I could find it, a second hand caught me under my arm and yanked me backward. I was dragged, still screaming, through the door behind me and into the fresh air of the night.

That had been the last room.

My friends stared down at me, half laughing, half crying. I laid in the dirt for a moment until a staff member came towards us. She looked mildly amused. She offered to take our tickets and punch the final hole in our completion card. We had done it. We had made it through all seven houses.

I was oddly proud of that moment. It was as though nothing could touch me. Nothing I have ever seen could be as scary as what we had to walk through in those houses. My moment of shining pride was brought crashing down around me when the guys reminded me that I only made it through because somebody pulled me out at the last moment.

They were right. Had I been able to, I would have run for that chicken exit as quickly as my legs would have carried me. In that moment of fear, it didn't matter what I was losing. No reward in my mind could have been worth the fear I was experiencing. Just for a minute, everything that I had worked for in the last few hours, all of the houses that I fought through, all that I had overcome, would not be worth the reward that I set out to get.

As I ate my pizza, I thought about what a profound feeling that was. To have come all the way through that struggle to give up on what I was fighting for. Had I been able to find that exit, you bet your bunions that I would have used it without question. It took help to pull myself out of that mindset. I had to lean into the promise of what I was looking for. It's not that I wanted to give up;

I just did not know that the end to that fight was so close.

That is not an uncommon occurrence at all in seasons of almost. It is so easy to become so jaded and complacent in our waiting, that the season itself begins to sound like a great place to settle. We give up on our goals and opportunity because we have lost sight of them in our fear. It is the same line of thinking that made me believe that the floor of a haunted house may be less scary than what was behind the next door.

Fear not only acts as a deterrent in our quest for understanding and purpose; It also acts as a distraction. It is easy to be blinded by the feeling of desperation and despair around us if we cannot keep our eyes fixed on what led us to this point in our lives. In our seasons of almost, fear abounds. I would argue that fear is the very foundation of the uncertainty that we feel while in this season of preparation. There is nothing that the almost stretches us in more than our capacity to dispel fear. In a time where we are fighting fears of our self-worth, our circumstances, and our ability to grow, everything finds a root in its clutches. The only cure for fear is it's opposite;

Courage.

I am not talking about this concept in its contemporary form. Courage has been an entity that has been distorted for eons before my birth, and I'm sure it will continue long after my time. In movies, we see this characteristic portrayed in the invulnerability of our heroes. They are called fearless for rushing into situations that they had nothing to fear in any way.

Think about it. How much bravery would it take to rush into the battlefield knowing that you are immune to bullets? Not a whole lot if we're being honest. I would think much more of a perfectly mortal man putting his life on the line as they follow Superman into the battle than I would the "Man of Steel" himself. Yet this is the standard that I find that we hold ourselves to. We continue to look down at our character because we make decisions based on how fearful their outcome may make us. We are afraid to push forward because unlike Superman, we are not immune to the effects of the battle before us. The truth is we are not brave because we do not feel fear.

We are courageous because even in the face of our anxiety we make the choice to continue fighting anyway.

Fear, much like the idea of peace, is a choice. Choosing to live under the uneasiness that fear places us in, is allowing the despair to have power over our being. By pushing ourselves through the next door, we may be able to breathe freely in the breakthrough that is waiting for us on the other side.

The most unnerving thing about the almost, is the fact that we cannot see where the end is. It can feel as though we have been fighting for ages. Struggling to breathe free of the stress that this season can bring with it. Getting comfortable in our place of chaos can seem like our only option but wondering where that breakthrough was will always haunt our spirits.

The almost is not just a season of waiting. It is also a season of work.

This alone may seem like a shock. While the almost can feel like a bit of a holding tank, there are things that we can do in the meantime. The trick is that all of this work can seem futile when the reward for our work looks distant. If it seems like every door that we open is just another room full of fear, it can be easy to believe that fear is all that exists.

This is the greatest lie that the almost could tell you.

I am not sure of your background, or where you are coming from. I started this book by telling you that I knew you wouldn't find what you were looking for.

While all of this is true, there is one thing that I can promise.

You were created to live a life full of more than just fear.

You are meant to feel love and kindness. You were intended to feel whole and accepted. I know that this will be a difficult concept to grasp for some of us who have walked a darker path, but it's true. I promise you that the fear that you are feeling is temporary. It is just one more room on your journey. It is just as temporary as your season of almost. It is ok to stumble. It is normal to feel as though there is not a point to this.

It is not ok to give up.

You will get there someday, and when you do, I want to celebrate that breakthrough with you.
Keep pushing.

13.

There's Not a Funny Title For This One
And I'm Sorry

I got to go on an absolutely amazing spring tour a few years ago. We literally trucked up and down the country for months. Coast to coast and I got to eat In-N-Out for the first time in my life. At one point, we made a stop in a college town in Illinois. The band that I was with had been booked on a show that I was not able to play. Rather than work my way on to the lineup, I took the day off and came to support the other group.

After their show, I noticed that there were sign-ups for an open mic comedy event at the same venue for later that night. I had never done comedy before, but I figured if I just took the spoken word out of my spoken word set, that the jokes I had in between would suffice. I jotted my name down for the first slot. I figured if I completely bombed then maybe nobody would be there early enough to see it.

As seems to be the pattern for this book, I was wrong. There were plenty of people there. In fact, the house was packed. To make it worse, the comedy sets were being live-streamed to a few hundred viewers. They would be able to react live over the video feed as I was talking. They were also known for being unforgiving in their feedback, which, luckily for me, was being projected on to the wall in real-time.

When the emcee called my name, the crowd waited for me to begin. I talked about my kitchen fires and my grandmother. I'm pretty sure I also threw in a "Rick and Morty" joke for flavor. As my time was coming to an end, I realized that I didn't have a way to end my comedy set. Usually, if I'm doing my spoken word, the video and tracks take care of that for me.

Here, there was no production to hide behind. Once I ran out of jokes, I just kind of sighed and looked back out at the crowd.

I realized that we as a collective humanity have certain behaviors that mask how we are feeling. I knew that there were a lot of comedians in the room and that we make jokes to cheer people up. The problem is that sometimes we use the same jokes to mask that we are hurting.

I walked into that venue in pain. Not physically, although being in a cramped van for weeks was certainly no help. I'm talking about a deeper type of aching that just magnifies the uncertainty of the almost. This is the type of pain that comes from the feeling of betrayal and anger that comes when another person hurts you deeply. The type of pain that time doesn't dilute and who's effects can cause lasting damage to your ability to trust others.

I sat for weeks trying to think of a way to talk about the most sensitive part of the almost. This chapter has caused me more headaches than finals week in high school. It is the most personal part of this book, and easily the hardest. I ran ideas through my head for hours, thought of stories, and tried to come up with a funny chapter title. For awhile I convinced myself that I was only worried about the coherency of this book.

I thought that I had to start it with a funny memory or some anecdote. That there had to be some humor to it in order to keep the same pattern as all of the chapters before this one. What I was trying to come up with though, a way to soften the subject matter. I was fighting another mask. It was another thing that would stand between us, and pure vulnerability. It was exactly what I promised you at the start of this journey that I would not do.

That story about the night at the comedy open mic is one that is filled with what I was trying to avoid. Even remembering what led me to that tour in the first place was difficult. Embracing the pain and learning to heal from it though, is the last thing that I needed to do to overcome my season of almost. Once I confronted this fact, there is no getting around it.

This chapter is going to hurt, and I'm sorry.

What's worse is that it's not going to be what I'm writing that's going to hurt you. The pain that it's possible you are about to experience was already inside of your heart. All this chapter is going to do is make you face it. Remember though, we promised each other honesty and vulnerability in the hope that healing would happen. We cannot begin healing without acknowledging the wound.

Pain is a powerful feeling. It is the mixture of so many other emotions and seasons. It can be hard to place. When it does show up however, you can't ignore it. It eats at everything that you do and gnaws through the distractions that you put in its way. It has the ability to hold your peace hostage. It can take away every good thing you've been able to accomplish and, in the meantime, tell you that nothing you have done matters. It consumes everything, making change impossible, and seasons of almost seem everlasting. The only way to begin to heal though is to feel it.

Feeling is an action that can be both intentional and unintentional. Intentionally digging through our emotions in order to weed out the negative or taxing ones can be a delicate process. It is made even more complicated by the emotions that are developed when we are hurt by the very institutions that are supposed to make us whole.

Even that sentence brought back memories for some of you that I'm so sorry you have to fight.

This chapter is for every forgotten child, every hurting person, and for those of us that have been forgotten in the war between holiness and grace. While the quest for purity tends to be a noble one, the causalities left in its wake are all too often disregarded.

If this is for you,
I'm sorry.

I am sorry that you have joined a club of hearts longing to be made whole again without direction. I apologize for the fact that in many cases those who are supposed to be the light in dark places turned out to be the shadows that hid hope from you to begin with. I'm sorry that you've had to deal with individuals that would much rather be right than reconciled.

It is easy in these instances to believe that forgiveness will lead to the dismissal of our pain. That suddenly, we will become forgotten the moment our grievances are relinquished. That we will lose our ability to be seen if we allow light to invade the darker corners of our hearts. Let me just say something to you.

I see you.

I believe you.

I value you more than I value your scars.

The road to healing is a long one. It involves seeing the shortcomings in others and overlooking our desire for justice. To let go of the anger that their actions have caused. In some cases, this can be nearly impossible. It is hard to overlook the wrongs of another when their consequences stare you in the face on a day to day basis. When your life, for however long, seems to be dictated by the choices that they've made against you. It can be hard to stop the bleeding from wounds that are both emotional and physical if you feel as though the person responsible is still cutting you.

Notice that I did say *nearly* impossible.

At the end of the day forgiveness, like peace, is a choice. By harboring malice in our hearts for those around us, we are simply allowing them to live rent-free in a space that happiness is also vying for. We can easily lose ourselves in the bitterness that pain invites and never hurt anyone other than ourselves.

Despite my optimism, I am not naive. I know that there are acts so heinous that forgiveness and closure can seem like distant concepts. In these cases, know that closure is a process. It does not happen overnight and anyone who says that it can is fooling themselves. Forgiveness allows us to close that chapter on our lives and begin living for something more. It allows us the freedom to continue searching for what we are looking for. This is easy when who we harbor unforgiveness against is human.

Did you know that we can have unforgiveness against God as well?

I fought and lost a battle with my car over the idea that being angry with God is possible. I know that it was easy to give in to that anger. However, I was not ready for the conversation about what my unforgiveness towards my Creator was doing to my relationship with Him. I also was not ready to admit that my issues with His sovereignty had nothing to do with Him at all. I had to come to grips with the fact that a lot of my anger and feelings of betrayal stemmed from the things that were done in His name.

Seasons of can almost be as much an opportunity for healing, as it is for forgiveness. We cannot continue to move in our calling if we are ignoring the Lord that is calling us. Until that conflict is resolved, we will continue following His plan for our lives out of obligation and not love. We project our anger towards His people at Him.

While I am sorry that your story has been tainted with pain, I want to encourage you to set aside placing blame. Just as we have to approach our anger with God in prayer, we also have to bring our unforgiveness to Him as well. It's not easy, especially if your view of Him has been replaced by a fragmented sense of love or a grace that is conditional. Understand that this is simply an obstacle. That feeling is another distraction from the only voice that has been pursuing you since the day that you were born. This process will take time, but don't worry.

This love can wait.

14.

I Tried to Write Song On A Beach In California. I Ended Up Writing a Poem About The State of Montana

It has always been a dream of mine to sit on a beach in California and write a song. Call it a musician's fantasy or a Switchfoot imitation, but it's been on my bucket list for a while. During a winter run, I got that chance. I refused to write anything in the weeks leading up to the tour. I'd supposed that I was hoping to be so pent up with creative energy that once I saw the ocean, it would all flow out in perfect harmony. That I'd have a number one billboard hit on my hands with nobody to thank but God, the academy, and the tide.

This is not what happened.

I did make it to San Diego though. We camped out by the beach for a few days while we explored the city. It was everything I could ever have dreamed for it to be. It was the middle of March and this kid from the upper Midwest was strolling around in shorts and a t-shirt. I'm pretty sure I sent my grandmother pictures just to make her jealous as she sat in the snow. Finally, the night came for the bonfire and I was ready to write.

First though, the tour took a field trip to the ocean. It was the first time I had ever seen the Pacific. I had seen the Atlantic of course, as well as the Gulf, but this was different. It was beautiful.

Did you know that beach bums are actual things?

I didn't. I'm not sure why I thought that they would be a fictitious thing in the first place. We don't have too many of those in Ohio, so the concept was a foreign one to me. We met one on the afternoon of the bonfire. He was incredibly kind and spent time talking to the adults of the group about the best places to catch some waves if ever we wanted to surf. He started talking about some cool tidepools and a privet beach that he had over on the other side of a cliff. We thanked him for his information and continued on with our day.

As the sun was setting, the group decided to head to the tidal pools that sat on a cliff near the spot that our friendly neighborhood beach bum had motioned too. What they did not mention was that in order to get there we would have to climb several fences and jump a few barricades labeled "KEEP OUT" in giant red letters. It was the most California thing I've ever done.

After a bit of a hike, we crested onto a giant shale overhang full of tidal pools. The view was breathtaking. The pier that we had just jumped over framed the view. The sun was setting. Everything was picturesque. I stood for a while just looking around and trying to take everything in. Waves were crashing 50 feet below us, but up here we seemed to be untouchable.

After a few minutes of exploring, our old buddy the beach bum came back towards us from just around the corner. He told us stories and legends about the area. I asked him about where he slept, and he pointed to the area he had motioned to earlier. Around the corner was a smaller beach, just like he had said. I could see a hammock, a fire pit, and some games that were set up. He mentioned that he didn't want anyone to think that he was a creep, but that he did enjoy seeing young people connect with the ocean as he had. That somehow, here felt more like home than any brick and mortar building ever could.

I thought a lot about that as we made our way back to the campfire. I was actually almost sad. While the other band was chattering excitedly about the day's adventure, here I was having an early life crisis. The concept of home always seemed like a weird one. As someone who has spent most of their life touring, it was hard to visualize. I mean, I have stayed in many people's homes. Eaten at promoter's houses, even been to the houses of other bands, but as I sat on the beach, I realized there wasn't really a spot that I could give that name to. I love Cleveland. I despise the snow, but my family is there. My cat and lizard even live there, and if something were to happen on this tour, that is where I would go to. The issue is that after you have traveled for a while, everything seems like a pit stop. Just another side trip on the way to your destination.

I'm just not sure what that destination is. If I was on tour, then I'd assume it would be a show, but shows end. Tours only run so long and then after that it's a waiting game for the next one. I was becoming restless even thinking about the end of the run I was on. I was struggling to find peace and stability in a job whose entire draw is the fluctuation.

I sat at the campfire with my pen in hand ready to channel the creativity that I had been trying to harness for weeks. I had come all the way across the country for this chance. There was literally no other place I could go in the US and be further from my house, and yet I wasn't sure where home was.

This is how I sat on a beach in San Diego and wrote an entire poem about the state of Montana.

To be clear, I've never actually been to Montana. However, the things that I have heard about it seem to always include some sort of adventure. It is a group of only 5 states that I have not yet toured through. To me, it symbolizes the wonder of a peace that I'm not sure I know yet. In a lot of ways, this is exactly what the almost is.

The almost is a place between where we are and where we want to be. Sometimes it is for a season of preparation, and in others it can be a season of struggle. We've covered what these concepts look like already, but the longing in the almost is hard to describe. I only know that Montana exists because I've seen it on a map. I could not begin to tell you how to get there, but I do know that it is, in fact, a real place. The concept of home is the same way.

It is also what hurts the most

Past the chaos, fear, and emotional desperation of the almost is the longing for home. In many cases, we believe that the longing in our season of almost is due to a lack of opportunity. We think that what we are really looking for is the next item in our long list of desires. Let me ask you something. If you were to write a list of everything that you are waiting for and hand it to me would your season of almost be over or just postponed? Would the aspirations of our hearts fill the holes in our souls or would it just create another temporary solution for an eternally based problem? If all of the fear in our lives were replaced with the stability that we seek, would our emotions turn to happiness or apathy? Is what we are looking for actually what we need or is it just another fish to distract us from our longing?

I don't care who you are or what you think you came here looking for. The reason that I was so confident that I would not be able to give you answers in this book is a simple one.

I cannot give you home.

What you are looking for is a place that we have never seen and only known through feeling. To be honest, I can't even define that in its entirety for you either. We have talked about some of its characteristics. We know that home is a place full of peace, courage, acceptance, encouragement, and In-N-Out. Even with all of those things combined we still would be left with an inadequate picture of what home is. Despite my inability to give you what you are really looking for, there are somethings that I know I can work to create.

Home is a place of peace, understanding, and grace. It is a spot where toxic varieties of shame have no place and where grace abounds. I cannot give you what you are longing for, but I can emulate its characteristics. Every morning we all wake up with the opportunity to act as signposts for the hope that we say we act on.

We have the chance to be the love that we say we believe in.

15.

This Is Almost The Ending
That You Were Expecting

Endings are hard. Endings without answers are harder. This book is about to give you both of those things. I started this with an apology. I promised you that you were not going to be able to find what you were looking for in these pages. That I was not going to be able to definitively hand you the exact thing that you needed to end your season of almost. While this was not a lie, it also was not entirely true.

The almost is a strange season. It exists for a variety of reasons. Its end is not a simple matter of saying a few magic words. It is not as easy as waiting for an opportunity or for the chance to try. The end to the season of almost is a shift in mindset. It is looking into the face of uncertainty with the determination that comes from the confidence in the promise of a better tomorrow. It is not being stuck in the wait; it is being prepared for the journey. Despite the waning number of pages in this book, you should know something;

This is not the end.

This may be the end of this chapter of your life. It may be the end of another season of waiting. It may be the start of a new adventure. You may be looking at a time of closure or the finale in a long line of not so great events. You may be on your last nerve because someone is using it as a jump rope. The truth is that the almost is a process. It is not something that can be completed and moved away from. While its emotional effects can be profound, they are not enduring. Understand that this fact also comes with a promise. While this might be the end of this particular season, know that the following is also true.

This is not the end of you.

I know that I have not had the chance to meet all of you. Those of you that I have met have been nothing short of inspiring. Your stories are reminders that there is hope in every sunrise and redemption in every song. It is insanity to think that so much beauty can come out of backgrounds so dark.

Yet, you are still here.

It is impossible to fathom the innate human ability to not just survive but thrive under the darkest circumstances. You, yes you, are proof that it is possible to overcome adversity and pain to grow. You are confirmation that darkness cannot exist without the light. That the difference between defeat and victory is a choice, and that peace is accessible even in the chaos. That despite having every reason to give up, the glow that radiates from your triumph evident. I do not know you, but I also don't have to. I know that behind every face there is a story. It may be one of triumph, pain, or struggle, but it will always be a story worth telling. Powerful in nature, and divine in purpose. You have taught me one thing;

Hope persists.

It is not a lost opportunity, not a failed venture, or misplaced longing. It may be concealed now, but in time it will push its way past your walls and shove you into a season of healing. It promises that our scars are still covered under grace. That time does not diminish its power. Hope shows me the only constant in the season of almost.

Love is patient.

Too many times I feel as though people forget this. Depending on the background, it is possible for a person to believe that love is transactional. Only accessible via favors or deeds. That it is out of reach for those with too little to give, and too much to hold on to. Our baggage weighs on our conscience and slows our journey through a season that demands our understanding. It drags our hope through its instability and into a place where we feel like we are not worth its gift. It traps us into a circle of fear that we no longer feel worthy of escaping. For some of you, that paragraph hit a little too close to home. While you did promise me your honesty, you did not think about the fact that your emotions would be susceptible to review. That the memories locked in your closet may try to force the lock you've latched them under.

Understand that it is ok to feel.

Sometimes that feeling is nothing. Sometimes it is everything at once. It can be a mess, but the healing that follows is worth the snot that will precede its invasion on your heart's crawlspaces. Allow the compartmentalized regions of your being to let the light in. Let it wash out the secrets and pain that you have been holding onto, believing that it was the last thing worth waiting for.

Peace is possible.

I also believe that you are worth it. Worth the stability that hope, love, and healing bring. That you deserve all of the peace that is possible to have. I may not know the exact details of what you are dealing with, but I don't really need to. If that pain is rooted in mistakes, abuse, embarrassment, or the simple need to start over I believe that you are worth that chance. I know that the hope you are craving is accessible, even when you do not believe it for yourself.

"Hallelujah nevertheless,
was a song that pain couldn't destroy"
– *Joy Invincible*
Switchfoot

You probably skipped right over this part, but this lyric was on one of the first pages of this book. It is one of my favorite lyrics, to one of my favorite songs, by one of my favorite bands. If you have ever heard of Switchfoot, then you already know exactly what I'm talking about. If you've not yet had a chance to see them, you officially have homework. I've been going to their shows purposefully since about 2012 after discovering them on accident as a child. The story of what led me to their concert is probably enough to fill another book. Regardless of origin, their lyrics have the ability to be simultaneously uplifting and incredibly heavy. This lyric is a great example of that.

On the surface, the line sounds pretty simple. On the record, the track is sandwiched between a really cool rock and roll ballad and one of the most heart-wrenching songs I have ever heard. The track itself is a cross between an atmospheric rock song and techno-pop melody. It grapples with finding joy in dark places. Not just finding it, but holding on to it in the wait. I never realized what a heavy topic the lyrics touched on until I saw the song performed live. Maybe it's just me overcomplicating things. Maybe Jon Foreman just has a thing for incredibly profound lyrics.

I'm going to say that it's probably both.

Whatever the reason, I see two different ways to view the meaning of these lyrics. To be fair, I have also not had the chance to ask how this lyric is supposed to be read. Then again, knowing this band, they probably mean both interpretations at the same time. For me though, it all depends on where the emphasis is placed in the wording. For example:

"**Hallelujah** nevertheless,
was a song that pain couldn't destroy"

Hallelujah

Interjection

[hal-*uh*-**loo**-y*uh*]
1. an exclamation of "hallelujah!"
2. a shout of joy, praise, or gratitude.

With an emphasis placed on the exclamation, this phrase takes on a more joyful tone. In seasons of stability, this can be a welcomed variation of the lyrical meaning. As a Christian, I can see this as a form of worship. Thanking my Creator for the work that He has done by using a word that typically designates a divine nature to the one being praised. During periods where joy comes as second nature, it is easy to give praise in moments of strength. It is good to understand that all ordained times and seasons come from above. It is effortless to point to a God who promises His love when His blessings are evident.

In the event that this is the lens that this song is being looked at in, the "hallelujah" is the most important term. It has become the center of all celebrations and happiness. This view is only easy to hold onto in seasons of joy. This song becomes a celebration brought on by the promise that the singer is walking in. When seasons of uncertainty present themselves, it's not that simple.

"Hallelujah **nevertheless,**

was a song that pain couldn't destroy"

Nevertheless

[nev-er-*th uh*-les]

adverb

1. nonetheless;
2. notwithstanding;
3. however;
4. in spite of that:
5. *But*

This is my favorite interpretation. With the emphasis placed on the second word of this lyric, everything changes. The focus of the joy experienced is no longer on the evident celebration. It is now focused on the perseverance of the singer. It now means that regardless of circumstance, the story being told is now a story that pain could not eradicate. That the struggle was not overcome by the power of shame. That in spite of the clouds, light persevered. That despite the seemingly insurmountable evidence to the contrary, joy is still possible. That even in all of the vague struggles we sing about, the mountains that we have defined have been defied by the weight of the power that is coming behind us and pushing us through. That pain almost defeated our defenses, *but* love persisted.

Almost

[awl-mohst, awl-mohst]

Adverb

1. very nearly;

2. all *but*

This is not the resolution that you were expecting. It is impossible to tie all that has been discussed here into a neat little bow and call it complete. Doing so would be a lie. It's simple really. This is not over, because this season is not finished.

We are not complete.

Thankfully we don't have to be. It is ok to be messy. That is what the almost is. It is a process. It is this swath of uncertainty, emotion, longing, and fear that every human being goes through. The moment that defines our transition out of the almost, and into our journey though, is one that can be quickly overlooked in its absence. It can be easily discarded in our haste for closure. Your ticket out of the almost is very simple. In fact, it is what you came to this book looking for.

Hope.
You are looking for hope.

Getting lost in the almost is a simple as losing sight of what it is you are searching for. We replace our need for reason with our desire to be "doing". We become wrapped up in our task list and its status of completion. In that mindset, we forget that our lists are only substitutes for our real need.

We patch the holes in our carpets with temporary mats. We scream at our cars with the same level of impatience at our faulty repairs. We become surprised at the chaos we have been tossed into in pursuit of something that only breeds discontent. We get pulled head over heels into a lake of opportunity that we were never meant to navigate on our own, but become agitated when we come up empty. Chasing a whisper of purpose through mountains and yet we still end up surprised that we got lost along the way, deafened by our need for a quick solution rather than an eternal one.

We are so scared by our inability to solve the holes in our hearts that we remain frozen in fear just in front of our breakthrough. All before replacing our need with a synthetic stand-in, given to us by someone who did not create us in the first place. All of this, while what we are looking for is on a map in front of us, but is being confined by our inability to read directions.

We have all gotten lost in a season of almost.

It's easy when we get so distracted by all of the things that we can't find. It took one hundred and thirty-three pages to get to a point where we could collectively understand this.

But we are here now.

There has never been a better time than this exact moment to locate the hope you came here looking for. I believe that you are worth, and worthy of the same joy, peace, and hope that we have been talking about over these last few pages. I have no idea where you are coming from, but I know that you are worth more than your scars. I care for you more than the walls that you've built and more than the mistakes that you have made. If nobody has ever said this before, then understand that I mean this in earnest.

I am so happy that you are here.

Not just here reading this book. I am happy that you are alive. I am happy that you, a walking story, have found the strength to fight against all of the things that have reared up against you. That you have become the epitome of a song that pain could not destroy. You have fought and bested your fears and are coming into your own. While I do admire your strength, I want to tell you too, that you do not have to struggle alone.

We have been honest with each other. For the last one hundred and thirty-four pages, you have walked in a vulnerability that is expectant of a season of healing. The catch is that I cannot do the rest for you. I cannot make you believe, force you to see, or coerce your heart into changing. This next part is something that will require a skill that we have not brought up yet.

Here, you'll need faith.

What if I told you that the hope you are looking for has a name? That the love it is reaching out towards you with has and will always be a gift. That we cannot earn this any more than we deserve the peace that it brings. That this love has been pursuing you with the same persistence and passion that it has had since the day that you were born? Did you know that this love has a name?

His name is Jesus.

Now hold on just a second. I head half of you started shouting that hallelujah word we were just talking about, and the other half of you groan.

Trust me, I get it.

Like I said, this is not the end you were expecting to a book that cannot give you what you're looking for. I know that His name can carry a weight that was not intended. Some of you may be dealing with a feeling of doubt. Some of you may be dealing with the scars of wounds caused in the name I just promised would bring you peace. Then again, some of you are just coming from a feeling of jadedness towards religion in general. I want to invite you, regardless of your background, into a relationship. I'm not trying to convert you into a religion, not pushing an agenda, and no I'm not going pass around an offering plate at the end of this paragraph. I just truly believe that you are worth the peace that comes from a relationship with the healer of souls Himself. Take that for what you will or leave it until you're ready. Just know that this invitation is open, it's free, and it has been waiting for you to come home.

So, this is really it huh?
The end of this book.

Maybe it is. Maybe this is just the start of something more. The start of a new relationship. The beginning of a new chapter. The end to the season of waiting that some of us have been wading in. Whatever it is though, I am glad that you are here. I am proud of the person you are fighting to be, and I cannot wait to celebrate with you once you get to where you are going.

We have faced the storms and overcome their swells. We have fought through our chaos and have held steady to our peace. Through our honesty, we have found ourselves to be halfway there. Our vulnerability will lead us home. Our healing will make us whole. The hope that we have found will come to stay.

We are just about home.

Almost anyway.

An Open Letter To My Village

One of my grandmother's favorite sayings is that "It takes a village to raise a child". As this work comes to a close, I cannot help but agree. When I sat down to write this book, I was overwhelmed with feelings, ideas, emotions, and experiences. Sorting these thoughts here was as much an exercise in grammatical competency as it was a journey to healing. To say that what is contained in these pages is entirely my doing could not be further from the truth. I have been blessed with some incredible people in my life. I am confident that if I were to take the time to thank all of them individually that there would be enough stories to fill a whole other book.

For now, know that I am beyond thankful for each of you. Thank you for letting me come and hang out at a session, for answering my questions, letting me play with your stuff, and listening to my 2 am rants that either sounded like coherent philosophical musings or the ramblings of less than sane human being. Thank you for showing me what love looks like and how to produce from a posture of worship. Thank you for taking in this pint-sized poet and showing me all that is possible and explaining things I never could have dreamed of. I am so humbled to have you in my village. I am honored by the fact that you would share your time with me. Thank you for the privilege of calling you friend. To my village, you have shaped, changed, and pushed me farther than you know.

You know exactly who you are.
Thank you for being you.

About the Author

Egypt Ali is a spoken word artist from Cleveland, Ohio. At the age of 16, Egypt placed nationally in the Fine Arts competition, earning her the rank of 1st in the state of Ohio and 2nd in the country in the art of spoken word. Professionally known as Egypt Speaks, she released her first full-length album independently in 2016. After the record's release, Egypt began touring the country sharing stories of hope with audiences of all ages. While recent years have found her gaining recognition for her work in studio production, poetry, and her accidental incidents of pyromania, Egypt finds the most joy in playing her guitar. When she is not on the road, she enjoys spending time reading, writing music, watching football, and hanging out with her cat and lizard.

Learn More At:
egyptspeaksofficial.com

Made in the USA
Middletown, DE
29 February 2020

85322538R00104